PEN AND PLOUGH

Pen and Plough

Diarmuid Johnson

First published in 2016

Published with the financial support
of the Welsh Books Council

ISBN: 978-1-84527-591-4

Cover design: Eleri Owen
Picture: Sebastian McBride

Published by Gwasg Carreg Gwalch,
12 Iard yr Orsaf, Llanrwst, Wales LL26 0EH
tel: 01492 642031
email: books@carreg-gwalch.com
website: www.carreg-gwalch.com

Er cof am nhadcu John Walter Morgan
a mamgu Sarah Ellen Morgan (née Jones)

Contents

Preface

I began reading the work of the Ceredigion bards and poets on my return to Wales in 2002, having left as a child in 1968. In 2008 while Guest Professor of Celtic Studies in Poznań, Poland, I began to formulate some of the ideas that underpin *Pen and Plough*. With the deaths in 2009 of John Roderick Rees, Dic Jones, and T. Llew Jones, and in 2011 of W.J. Gruffydd, the fact that an era had ended prompted me to undertake an in-depth study of a rich heritage that risked falling into oblivion. A knowledge of other traditions, and time spent over the decades in other countries – Ireland, Brittany, Poland, and Romania – enabled me to approach the corpus in a way that had not been done before.

Some of the material in *Pen and Plough* has been presented to public and academic audiences in Wales, Ireland, Germany, Poland and Norway. A writer's residency in 2014 in Rhos-y-Gilwen House, North Pembrokeshire, afforded me time to develop a framework for the book. I hope the work will serve the Welsh tradition well, and attract interest not only in Ceredigion, but further afield, in Britain and Ireland, on the European continent, and in other parts of the world.

I would like to thank my family for their support, the Irish Government who funded a post for me in Bonn University in 2013, Ystwyth Books, Aberystwyth, where I found most of the books in the bibliography, and my wife, friends and colleagues who read the manuscript and offered me their valuable advice.

Diarmuid Johnson, Y Borth 2016

Foreword

This is a remarkable interpretation for a wider audience of a remarkable phenomenon – a body of verse composed in Welsh by poets within the agricultural community in Ceredigion, and mainly *for* that community, during the second half of the twentieth century.

While some of the individual poets have found their way into the canon of Welsh poetry, too little attention has been paid to a body of work which taken as a whole is an important literary, cultural and historical record of a recently vanished world. Through the voices of their own poets, here sensitively paraphrased into English, we see the faces and enter the lives of those communities.

The great strength of Diarmuid Johnson's study is that while he works closely with the detail of individual poems and their place in the Welsh poetic tradition, he is at the same time able to set his subject within the wide comparative context of a European rural civilization which extended from Romania to Ireland. It is this comparative approach which also enables him to identify the unique features of a body of work for which he feels a strong sympathy.

Ned Thomas

Introduction

I

This book is an exploration of aspects of social, economic, and cultural change in Ceredigion, West Wales, during the 20th century, as documented in selected verse written and composed by bards and poets born into the farming community of the time. All the original work discussed here was composed in Welsh. The book concentrates on the publications of a dozen or more of the most accomplished authors of the period. All of the texts referred to are derived from collections of poetry that appeared in book-form between 1933 and 2011. Given that the original material is written largely in a sophisticated idiom and in complex bardic metres, a policy of loose paraphrase of the work has been adopted in these pages. Selected translations of the work of the Ceredigion bards will, it is hoped, appear in print at a time in the future.

Who are the Ceredigion bards of the 20th century? In *Pen and Plough*, the work of the following individuals is presented: Dafydd Jones (Isfoel) (1881–1968), Richard Davies (Isgarn) (1887–1947), Alun Jones y Cilie (1897–1975), B. T. Hopkins (1897–1981), J. M. Edwards (1903–1978), W. J. Gruffydd (1916–2011), John Roderick Rees (1920–2009), J. R. Jones Tal-y-bont (1923–2002), Dic Jones (1934–2009), and also Dewi Emrys (1881–1852), Dafydd Jones Ffair Rhos (1907–1991), and Evan Jenkins Ffair Rhos (1895–1959), T. Llew. Jones (1915–2009) and S. B. Jones y Cilie (1894–1964). With the exception of Dic Jones (1934–2009), all were born between 1880 and 1925. Details of their books are given in the bibliography. Typically, these men left school by the age of fourteen or so, and spent their lives on the land where their art and their tradition is rooted.

The work of the Ceredigion poets in the 20th century might very easily have remained unpublished and forgotten. The Welsh bard belongs to a tradition that is strongly oral in nature. Since the beginnings of the tradition in early medieval times, his work has been sung for a close-knit audience. His role is to record events that affect the community, to celebrate joyous occasions, and with his words to provide solace on funerary occasions. His work marks the passage of time within his community, is a record of the community's history, and becomes part of the community's identity.

The Welsh bards of Ceredigion composed verse, and often wrote it down, but rarely collected or anthologised it. Verse in Ceredigion was written on the stable door, on cigarette packets, on an old bill, or anything else that came to hand. Verses were cited from memory decades after composition, and the complex rhyming patterns used by the bards enabled them to store their verse in their minds. However, in the late 19th century, with the advent of the modern world in West Wales, and its diversity and mobility, this tradition could no longer function no longer as before. Without a well-defined audience, regularly exposed to recitation of verse, none would remember the work once its authors had passed on.

The efforts of a handful of activists in West Wales ensured that this did not happen. Prosser Rhys was born in Trefenter near Tregaron, and left his native area to pursue a career in journalism and publishing. In 1928 he founded Gwasg Aberystwyth Press, a publishing house influential in the 1930s that helped nurture the literary culture of the day in West Wales and beyond. Cymdeithas Lyfrau Ceredigion, (The Books Society of Ceredigion) founded in 1954 was also crucial to the nurturing of this culture, and was fuelled by the energies of men such as T. Ll. Stephens, a school-teacher from Talgarreg in the south of the county. More than any other perhaps, T. Llew Jones from the Llandysul area in the Teifi Valley, encouraged the local bardic community to publish their work, edited the manuscripts, wrote prefaces, and bridged the gap between farmyard and bookshop. Gwasg Gomer Press in Llandysul pursued a policy of publishing local writers, and so in the third quarter of the 20th century much of the corpus that forms the basis of this study found its way into print.

Several commentators have written with understanding about the work of these bards and others like them. Cited in *Teulu'r Cilie* (*The Cilie Family*) by Jon Meirion Jones, an article entitled 'A Member of an Older Breed' by critic, playwright and activist Saunders Lewis compares modern poets is to the traditional bard, *bardd gwlad,* or folk poet. 'These are the heirs of Taliesin, of the courts of Llywelyn the Great, of the country house poets of the 15th century' (p. 258). There is further reference to Saunders Lewis' article in the chapter *The Politics of Poetics.*

In her introduction to *Ail Gerddi Isfoel* (Isfoel's Second Volume), Margaret Jenkins sums up the role of the '*bardd gwlad*', the 'folk poet', as follows: 'Here is the chronicle of a part of the country rich in character, and of a society rich in character, of the adventures and misadventures of its people, their everyday troubles and worries, their sorrows, their bereavements and their moments of joy'. Margaret Jenkins' comments on the craft of the bard are perfectly in tune with Welsh culture: 'An artist is someone who makes *things,* whether he fashions a blade for a scythe, carves a wooden spoon, turns a pair of horseshoes, works wood to make a particularly beautiful cupboard or dresser, or indeed composes verse – *englyn* and *cywydd* – or song. Significantly, we speak of 'carving' verse, and here we delve deep into the meaning that surrounds the work of the artist'. These ideas are developed in the chapter on *Craftsmen*.

Amongst the older poets or bards whose work is discussed in these pages, those born in the late 19th century, there is no sense of ambition or self-importance whatsoever. The bard is a member of the community, an important member, but seeks no recognition. This is illustrated well in the short foreword Isfoel writes to his *Ail Gerddi* in 1965: 'I would like no-one to think that I strive to attain a literary standard of any sort as do the younger, modern poets of today'. In the foreword to his first collection on the other hand, Isfoel points out that influential academic works by such scholars as the great John Morris-Jones were 'well known amongst us', a reference to his brothers and the local bardic society of the day. Isfoel's standards, and those of his bardic brethren, were as rigorous as any, within their own critical framework, but they remain modest, and are content to serve the community, as their predecessors had done from medieval times and early modern times.

In *The Agricultural Community in South-West Wales at the turn of the 20th Century* (1971), David Jenkins summarises literary activity in Southern Ceredigion during the 18th and 19th centuries: 'In the later seventeenth and early eighteenth centuries the minor gentry were patrons of, and contributed to, the literary activity of Southern Cardiganshire and the Teifi Valley generally. The Lewes family of Gernos were patrons while Erasmus Lewes (d. 1745), educated at Jesus College, Oxford, was an active contributor. John Bowen, Esq., grandfather of the Revd. Thomas Bowen (d. 1842) of Troedyraur House, wrote a type of verse that was characteristic of south-west Wales in his day'. Jenkins continues: 'Stephen Parry, Esq. (d. 1724), of Neuadd Trefawr and Walter Lloyd, Esq., of Coedmor were both patrons of a volume of translations from the English made by the Revd. Alban Thomas (c. 1650–1734) of Blaen-porth, himself of gentle birth, whose other work provided one of the earliest titles to be printed on the first printing press to be established in Wales, at Atpar, Newcastle Emlyn, in 1718'. The following seminal statement serves to end this quote from Jenkins' book: 'From these men's plebeian contemporaries (e.g. Ifan Gruffydd, Twrgwyn, (c. 1655–1735), and Siencyn Thomas of Cwmdu (1690–1762), a continuous chain of culture-bearers can be traced down to the present day'.

II

Is the body of work to hand unique in European literature in the 20th century? It would seem that nowhere else in a rural setting in Europe has a body of work as rich and abundant been published in as short a time by so many accomplished poets. In 20th century Ireland, poets issue of rural communities wrote of life on the land; Patrick Kavanagh, John Montague, Séamas Heaney and Máirtín Ó Direáin, to name but four of many, but did so having moved on to other environments, urban as a rule. Other European traditions tell us less still of the rural space.

Germany offers occasional insight into the rural world, but from romantic to modernist times, this world is far from being a major focus of the tradition, whether in the work of Goethe, Hölderin, Schiller or others. An exception in 19th century German is Johann Peter Hebel of Basel, and in the

20th century Lena Kromer of Obereggenen. Beyond Brittany, Celtic in culture, in the work of Paul Keineg, for example, regionalism in the French lyric tradition is rare. In Poland, literary activity outside Krakow, Breslau and Warsaw is secondary to say the least. Further east, in Romania, in the work of Lucian Blaga, Tudor Arghezi and George Coşbuc, there is a tradition comparable in ways to Welsh, though here the literary language is established far later, Mihai Eminescu (1850–1889) being regarded as the father of the modern idiom, while Romanian as a language remained unwritten until the 16th century. In England, gentleman poets come and go, while others, Thomas Hardy for example, write of life in the rural space, but, unlike the poets of Ceredigion, they did not drive the plough themselves, nor are they members of a community of local writers who share a long tradition.

These ideas are developed further in the chapters *Idiom and Classical Language* and *Four Views of the Rural Space.* Two points suffice here. Firstly, the common people of Europe, until the last quarter of the 19th century, and often far later, spoke dialects that were rarely committed in an organised or sustained way to paper. These dialects and regional forms of speech were gradually replaced by standard national languages, French, German and Spanish, for example, from the late 1800s until our own day. This is not the case in the Celtic world where classical medieval language informs the modern culture. Secondly, the principal orientation of European culture is towards urban and metropolitan centres of learning and publishing, where writers, artists and intellectuals have gathered since before the time of the French Revolution to exchange and promote their ideas. In European literature, from 1800 until our own time, human activity in the rural space is marginal.

Regarding the continuity of the tradition from medieval

to modern times in Welsh culture, four lines by Dic Jones bring us to the heart of the matter. In *Storom Awst* (*August Storm*), he writes to welcome the National *Eisteddfod* to Cardigan where in 1176, in Cardigan Castle, Rhys ap Gruffydd hosted a gathering of bards called *eisteddfod*. In this poem, Dic Jones describes how the castle-grounds are derelict, and adds that there is no remnant of the pomp that once reigned there. Be that as it may, he continues, in certain farmhouses in the surrounding area, poetic inspiration still finds sanctuary today: a reference to 1976, the year the National *Eisteddfod* was held in Cardigan town.

III

From the time of the building of the great cathedrals in the 12th century until the industrial revolution in the 19th, a period seven hundred years long, European culture was largely agrarian, a peasant culture, a culture that revolved around the Christian faith, its feasts and rituals, together with the year's work as dictated by the land and the seasons. In the space of a few short generations in our era, this culture collapsed, and since the Second World War, with some exceptions in remote parts of Eastern Europe, it has now disappeared.

The disappearance of this rural culture is the subject of a book by French sociologist Henri Mendras called *La Fin des Paysans* (*The Last of the Peasantry*). When the book first appeared in 1967, it was greeted with some reserve. He introduces his book (p. 28) with the following statement, highly relevant to *Pen and Plough*: 'The study we are undertaking is that of the disappearance of traditional peasant civilisation, a fundamental constituent of western civilisation and Christianity, and of the replacement of it by the new technical civilisation.' In 1984, *La Fin des Paysans* was reprinted with a post-face in which Mendras, his thesis vindicated, now writes: 'in the space of a generation, France has seen the disappearance of a civilisation a millennium old'. The loss of peasant culture in France is a loss experienced across the European continent.

Where can evidence of this lost culture be found? Where has it been recorded? If one looks to the literatures of the major European languages, there is little of it to be found there. These languages are largely the idioms of the modern nation-state, not of the traditional provinces, regions and cultural areas of the European space. To find evidence of pre-industrial, rural culture in the literary tradition, we must find a place where this culture is described in an established literary idiom. This can be found in Wales, and more specifically, in West Wales, in Ceredigion. The *Conditions for the Emergence of the Tradition* and *Jeremiah Jones and the Making of the Tradition* are two chapters in which some the reasons for this are set out.

The word 'civilisation' is introduced above by Mendras, and it also occurs in the work of Breton writer Pierre Jakez Hélias. In *Le Quêteur de Mémoire* (Éditions Plon, 1990 p, 203), referring to the story-tellers in Breton tradition, Hélias writes: 'But today, and most specifically since the end of the Second World War, the decay has accelerated to such an extent that we are witness to the final hours of those who best represent our Old Testament. And the story-tellers are the first victims of this rapid development for the very reason that they, more than any, bore the hallmark of our distinctive civilisation before uniformity cast its lethal net'.

The detailed recording, from within, of aspects an old way of life now all but extinct in Europe, is one part of the legacy the 20th century Ceredigion bards. Another, equally rich, is the detailed recording of the transition from the older culture, pre-industrial and perennial, to the newer, mechanised and ambitious. This transition is dealt with in a chapter entitled *The Mechanisation of Agricultural.* Here, the disappearance of the horse from the farmyard, and its replacement by the tractor, is a theme visited and revisited by the Cilie brothers, Dafydd (Isfoel) and Alun Jones. In other chapters, *Women in the Corpus* and *Welsh Faces of Their Time,* for example, we identify certain social and economic changes parallel and related to those brought about by the mechanisation of agriculture. Religion plays its role in forming and defining Welsh culture during our period, and the 20th century begins in Ceredigion, and elsewhere in Wales, with a surge of spiritual fervour in 1904 and 1905, this coinciding with a virulent temperance movement, both of which we consider, briefly, in *Utopia and Dystopia.*

IV

The work presented in *Pen and Plough* is work published largely in the third quarter of the 20th century. Much of it is work written earlier in the century. This work represents one chapter in the long tradition of rural poetry in Wales, and images of ploughing occur in Welsh poetry from the earliest times. In his *Yr Aradr Gymraeg* (*The Welsh Plough*) (University of Wales Press, 1954), Ffransis Payne reminds us (p. 51) that in *Canu Llywarch Hen,* a cycle of poems from late in the first millennium, there are lines such as *pereid y rycheu, ny phara a'i goreu,* 'the ridges will endure, not so the hand that made them'. Some half a millennium later, in the 14th century, Iolo Goch in his *Cywydd y Llafurwr* (*The Labourer*), dedicates a long passage to the plough, also cited and analysed by Payne (pp 73-78), that includes details of the various parts of the plough.

Payne follows the history of the plough through to the 19th century, referring here to a ploughing competition, *Y Preimin,* named after a prize for agricultural excellence, the *premium,* instigated by Thomas Johnes of Hafod Uchtryd Estate, Ceredigion, in the late 18th century; 'The importance of the ploughing contest in the 19th century, y Preimin, cannot, it is evident, be overemphasised,' writes Payne (p. 136). 'In these competitions, the best ploughmen and ploughs from the surrounding areas were to be found vying for supremacy'. He notes, however (p. 138), that 'the local ploughs were first to disappear from 1918 on, the cause for this being the motor-car as much as the tractor. When the farmer left his horse-drawn cart aside to buy an automobile, the village blacksmith had one horse less to shoe. When a trailer was added to the car, the smith ceased to shoe a second. When a tractor was bought for the farm, the rest of the horses became redundant in most cases, and the blacksmith suffered yet another loss'.

Poetry is often a reflection of the world, of an environment at a given time in the world, and the society documented in *Pen and Plough* lived in an environment that had, as was the case in rural Britain in general, been shaped by events in the 19th century, none more so perhaps than the acts of enclosure. In *Cau'r Tiroedd Comin* (*Enclosing the Commonage*) (Gwasg y Brython, Liverpool, 1952), David Thomas provides us with the following information: 'In Wales, over a million acres of commonage was enclosed between 1795 and 1895. In 1795, some 35,000 acres having already been enclosed by twenty acts in the Senate, another 1,696,827 acres of commonage remained unenclosed in Wales according to the Agricultural Board – over a third of the entire surface of the country.' This acreage, explains Thomas, includes almost half the land in Ceredigion. In 1795, he says (p. 27), there were 206,720 acres of commonage in Cardiganshire while by 1895, there remained a mere 33,264 acres.

Referring to the costs of acquiring the right to farm former commonage, the obligatory fencing in of the land, for example, Thomas writes (p. 20): 'Very often, the costs would be higher than they [the tenants] could afford to pay, or the small-holding would lose all its value, having become too small to sustain a cow, and they would turn their backs on the countryside and migrate to the urban centres to look for work.' The theme of the enclosure of mountain commonage occurs in our corpus, and of migration, for various reasons, from the rural space towards centres of population. These themes are visited in two chapters, *Landlord and Tenant*, and *Four Phases in the Ownership of the Land.*

V

We have spoken briefly above of bards and poets, modern and traditional, the *prydydd* or verse-maker, the *bardd gwlad* or folk-poet. However, generic reference to any of these terms will tend to obscure the fact that behind each name there is a complex individual. There is no archetype in our corpus. There are parameters, as in all art. And there is diversity, just as in other artistic circles. The shepherd Isgarn observes the world from the margins. Hill-farmer B.T. Hopkins derives a cosmic vision from his life plying pen and plough. J.M. Edwards looks beyond the parameters, and risks despair. Dic Jones shines in the constellation, but is however only one of multiple reflections within the constellation. John Roderick Rees is the last of the smallholders. And blacksmith Jeremiah Jones, father of Isfoel, Alun Cilie, and S.B. Jones, is a catalyst whose energies helped to create the conditions in which a remarkable bardic society soon developed. These men and their work are treated in turn.

In *Pen and Plough,* the terms 'bard' and 'poet' are used alternately, the choice sometimes influenced by the tenor of the text in question. To understand the tradition, however, it needs to be addressed on its own terms. For this reason, two words are introduced here that play an important role in appreciation of the work. The first is *prydyddiaeth* and means 'verse-writing'. The *prydydd* is a 'verse-maker'. The second term is *barddoniaeth* and means 'poetry'. The *bardd* is a 'poet' or a 'bard', depending partly on his skill, and partly, for example, on his intentions while writing a given piece. In his autobiography, Dic Jones reflects on these terms (*Os Hoffech Wybod,* p. 131): 'Anyone who practices the sort of literature we usually call poetry is a *prydydd* ('verse-maker'). A small number of these verse-makers, who on occasion take flight, may elevate themselves to the rank of poet.' And he continues: 'Exactly where the boundary between the two lies is something I do not know'.

Wherever the boundary between verse-making and poetry may lie, it is crossed many times by the 20th Ceredigion bards and poets. *Ffenestri* (*Windows*) by W.J. Gruffydd is an unsung *tour de force* of rural realism comparable to Patrick Kavanagh's *The Great Hunger* in 20th century Ireland. Dic Jones' twin odes *Cynhaeaf* (*Harvest*) and *Gwanwyn* (*Spring*) are unsurpassed in the neoclassical tradition. However, the purpose of this book is not to create a literary canon. Closer to our aspirations is an investigation of a way of life, and a change in this way of life, as documented in the three thousand or so poems in our corpus. As has been seen, the themes of this major body of work include the end of the era of the landlord and the mechanisation of agriculture, but also seasonal migration to industrial Glamorganshire, the decline of shipping in Cardigan Bay, the demise of the Welsh chapels, and the arrival of English immigrants. However, the land, ownership of the land, and the community's relationship with the land, is the over-riding theme that drives the writing, as it informed and drove the lives of the people of Ceredigion and rural Wales.

With two simple quotes we conclude this introduction. The first is from Alun Cilie's first collection, and the poem *Cwm Tydu,* the name of the poet's beloved home, where he writes: 'Gone are the busy sounds of the grinding of the grain, gone the heat of the kiln fires'. And the second from *Llygaid* (*Eyes*) by John Roderick Rees of Bethania, from the collection *Cerddi Newydd 1983–1991: 'Cymysgiaith a chymysgwedd yw ein byd',* 'Our world is now a mosaic of faces and of tongues'. Nothing could be truer.

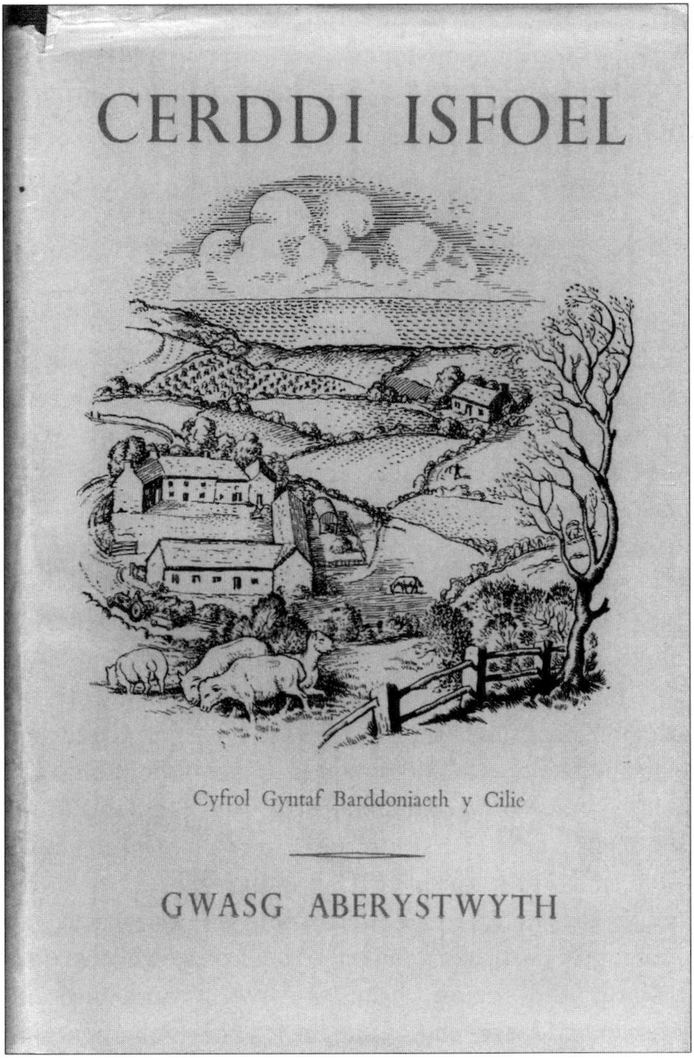
CERDDI ISFOEL
Cyfrol Gyntaf Barddoniaeth y Cilie
GWASG ABERYSTWYTH

PART I

THE TRADITION

THE EMERGENCE OF A LYRIC TRADITION: The Conditions for the Emergence of the Lyric Tradition in 20th century Ceredigion

The poetry of Ceredigion in the 20th century that forms the subject of this book was written in large part by members of the farming community, many of whom left school aged fourteen, and received little formal education in the conventional sense. How did it come about that such a sophisticated and abundant body of lyric work emerged in an isolated rural place in Wales in the 20th century? What conditions were in place for a tradition to reach such maturity far from the acknowledged literary centres of the world?

First we find that West Wales, in contrast to the valleys of South Wales, for example, remained relatively unindustrialised as the 19th century passed and the 20th century began. One result of this was that the society in Ceredigion remained traditional and rural, and the language strong. The mining industry was important to a degree, notably in the mountains near Ffair Rhos, near the source of the River Teifi, and also towards the Dyfi estuary in the north, but, unlike the valleys of South Wales, the region was not profoundly changed by the extraction work. Also, migration towards the region, from the Welsh midlands and Meirionnydd over the mountain towards Tal-y-bont and North Ceredigion, for example, tended to enhance the Welsh-speaking character of the society, and Welsh has remained the language of the native people in West Wales until this day.

The second condition that helped bring about the rise of sophisticated bardic schools was the annual local *Eisteddfodau,* or bardic gatherings, established around the county in Ceredigion from the late 1880s on. In a preface to *Caniadau Isgarn* (*The Songs of Isgarn*), S.M. Powell writes as follows of the shepherd Isgarn's dedication to the literary tradition: 'Isgarn received none of the advantages of education other than the years spent at the local primary school in Blaencaron. But for a man of his potential, the mountain and a shelf of selected books were magisterial teachers, and never did he miss a chance, hail or shine, to follow the literary movements and *Eisteddfodau* in Tregaron and Pontrhydfendigaid.'

In *Atgofion Dau Grefftwr* (*Two Craftsmen Remember*) by Dan Davies and William J. Hughes (Cymdeithas Lyfrau Ceredigion 1963), we are afforded a view of the preparations for a local *Eisteddfod* early in the 20th century: 'The tailor's workshop,' Dan Davies writes, 'must be kept warm, both in summer and in winter, to heat the smoothing iron. And in this warm atmosphere, people would come to seek company...And when an *eisteddfod* was to take place within a ten-mile radius [of Rhydlewis], the workshop would be the training ground for competitors in the recitation category, adults and children alike' (p. 44). In the *Eisteddfod* culture, all aspects of language, diction, grammar and expression, are rigorously instilled into competitors young and old.

The third factor that contributed to the flourishing of verse and poetry in the Welsh language in Ceredigion in the 20th century was the extra-mural evening classes organised at that time by the University of Wales, Aberystwyth, around the county. To quote again from S.M. Powell's preface to *Caniadau Isgarn*: 'he [Isgarn] would very regularly walk four miles through wind and rain to the extra-mural classes in Tregaron – especially to the excellent classes held by Prof. R.O. Davies on the mysteries of nature'. These classes were held in Welsh.

In a note of gratitude to his first volume of poems, *Rhwng Cyrn yr Aradr* (*Driving the Plough*), J.R. Jones acknowledges his debt to D. Gwenallt Jones, a figure of national importance in his day, with whom he studied for six years at extra-mural classes in Rhyd-y-Pennau, or Bow Street in English, a village between Tal-y-bont and Aberystwyth. J.R. Jones emphasises his 'great respect and admiration' for his teacher.

The Welsh literary tradition in general, and hence local tradition in Ceredigion, cannot be understood without reference to religious life in Wales. In *Coleg y Werin* (*The Common Man's College*), by Huw John Hughes, published by Cyhoeddiadau'r Gair (2013), we read that in the year 1718 a total of ten thousand copies of the Bible in Welsh were distributed free of charge by the SPCK (Society for the Protection of Christian Knowledge). In 1851, of a population of 97,614 people in Ceredigion, a total of 27% of these were in attendance at 287 Sunday schools in the county, no fewer than 25,000 students. The Sunday School remained an important institution in rural Wales throughout the 20th century, and its doors have not yet closed.

To appreciate the burgeoning of verse in the rural milieu in Ceredigion in the mid-20th century, and in this instance in South Ceredigion, the name Jeremiah Jones (1855–1902) merits attention. Aristocratic patronage of the bards in Wales decreased dramatically in the 16th century, but amongst the recesses where the old classical verse continued to be practiced was a place called Cwm Du in the parish of Brongwyn, near Newcastle Emlyn in Ceredigion. Jeremiah Jones, father of Isfoel, Alun Cilie and S.B. Jones, was descended from the bards of Cwm Du who practiced in the 18th century. In *The Agricultural Community in South-West Wales at the turn of the 20th Century* (p. 34), David Jenkins writes as follows about the 18th century bards of Cwm Du: 'Siencyn Thomas (1690–1762) was a shoemaker who had mastered the Welsh restricted verse measures. He was survived by three sons who wrote poetry. Of these Sion Siencyn (1716–96), also a shoemaker, composed verses to the gentry and frequented the competitive meetings (*eisteddfodau*) of his day. His brother Nathaniel Siencyn (1722–99) sang to *Palas Troed yr Aur*, that is, to the Bowens of Troedyraur House'. Born in 1855, the blacksmith Jeremiah Jones was of this lineage. His influence on the tradition is described further in the next chapter.

Living and working in a society with roots in the culture outlined briefly above, the work of the Ceredigion poets crystallises in a series of publications in book-form from 1947 when *Caniadau Isgarn* (*Songs of Isgarn*) was published, until 1986 when *Sgubo'r Storws* (*Sweeping the Storehouse*) by Dic Jones appeared. A flurry of publication between 1958 and 1965 constitutes as remarkable a seven-year period as any in the history of Welsh literature, a period during which numerous bards from Ceredigion published a selection of their life's work. With the death in 2009 of John Roderick Rees, Dic Jones and T. Llew Jones, and in 2011 of W.J. Gruffydd, these generations and the era they represented passed away.

yr
arloeswr
a cherddi eraill
DAFYDD
JONES

Literary Welsh – A Classical Language in a Rural Milieu

After the demise of the Roman Empire in Europe, the era of classical language is followed by the development of vernacular medieval languages across the continent. The modern romance languages are derived from the Latin source-tongue, and varieties of Germanic speech, including the Anglo-Saxon precursors of modern English, continued to establish themselves in their representative territories in Britain and, on the continent, east of the Rhein.

In the case of two Celtic languages, Welsh and Gaelic, things are somewhat different. From the 13th century on, building on earlier tradition, a classical idiom emerges in both countries, an idiom practiced by the bardic orders and literati of Wales, and of Gaelic-speaking Ireland and Scotland. In the latter territory, a huge swathe of land from the Hebrides in the north of Scotland to Munster in the south of Ireland, a rigorous written standard unites the territory for several centuries, until the time of Tudor expansion and the collapse of Gaelic civilisation in Elizabethan times. In Wales, in a somewhat smaller national territory from Monmouthshire to Anglesey, a classical literary language was also practiced for several centuries. This dichotomy involving the indigenous vernacular and a classical idiom existing in tandem is a feature of Celtic culture that does not occur elsewhere in Europe in the medieval world.

Three things define classical languages in general, and Welsh in this instance. One is the fact that they are written according to a strict standard that remains in place over a long period of centuries. Second is the fact that expression within the language is governed by numerous strict and complex conventions and rules, stylistic and grammatical. Third is the fact that this standard, stable and uniform, applies not only during an extended period of time, but is the standard used by a culture, or a civilisation, in a territory of significant size. Within this territory, the speech of the people may well vary from place to place, and evolve as time passes, but clarity of communication on a higher level is assured by the literary word.

While Classical Gaelic disappears quickly from Ireland early in the 17th century, and lingers in Scotland before expiring, the history of the literary language in Wales is somewhat more complex. In 16th century Wales, tensions grow between, on the one hand, a beleaguered bardic order doomed to extinction whose members insist on passing their knowledge down exclusively in the oral tradition, and on the other, the humanists of the day, who argue for transparency and modernisation. The Welsh Bible, a monumental work by Bishop William Morgan published in 1588, is a product of this time. To translate the Bible, William Morgan takes the several strands of older literary Welsh and weaves them into an idiom that becomes one of the foundations of modern Welsh writing. Also, unlike Ireland and Scotland where, owing to the turbulence of the times, the classical language could not persist, Wales witnesses the survival of its bardic idiom, albeit under conditions of compromise. In the 16th century therefore, classical Welsh goes underground, and its thread, though thin, continues to be spun in the work of an impoverished bardhood, re-emerging in the days of the modern *Eisteddfod* as the 19th century progresses. In this way, in the 20th century, classical Welsh finds its way into the poetry of Ceredigion.

Forms in classical Welsh poetry include the *cywydd*, *awdl* and *englyn*. The *cywydd* is a series of couplets, the *awdl* a form that features various bardic metres, and the *englyn* a four-line study. The line in classical Welsh metre is based on the syllable-count, not on the number of stresses, and each line and couplet are required to conform to the system of internal and end rhyme known as *cynghanedd,* a word that means *harmony.*

The lexicon of the classical bard includes literary synonyms for various phenomena. For example, the vernacular Welsh word for sea is *môr,* while in the lyrical language we find *gweilgi, heli,* and *lli.* The vernacular word for talking is *siarad,* while in poetry *ymddiddan* or *ymgomio* may be found. In vernacular Welsh, girl is *merch,* while in the bardic idiom *gwen, bun,* and *rhiain* all occur.

The literary language differs from the spoken language in its conjugation of verbs. Also, in Welsh classical poetry, the pronoun will invariably be omitted, while in the spoken language omission of the pronoun is unusual. In the spoken language, plural forms of the adjective are uncommon, while in the language of poetry these forms occur frequently. The literary language makes use of the infixed object pronoun, while the spoken language does not. Comparing a *cywydd* by a 20th century bard from Ceredigion, Isfoel for example, to a *cywydd* by Dafydd ap Gwilym who, like Chaucer, wrote in the 14th century, there are a host of similar features and characteristics. In Welsh, the richness of the tradition may be explained in part by its long history, and by the continuum it enjoys from medieval to modern times.

Unlike their predecessors in the 14th and 15th centuries however, the rural poets of Ceredigion and Wales in the 20th century also practice a number of other forms that occur in other languages from the 16th until the 19th centuries. Couplets and quatrains comprising accentuated lines with end-rhyme are a staple form. The sonnet is common in the corpus. Free verse, however, occurs seldom in the work of the Ceredigion poets before 1960. In a global context therefore, as regards form, the tradition is particularly conservative.

Here we compare briefly the metres used in three relevant volumes. The first by *Caniadau Isgarn* was published in 1949. The second is *Cerddi Alun Cilie* (1964), and the third *Caneuon Cynhaeaf* by Dic Jones (1969). Isgarn, the oldest of the three, uses the syllabic and accentuated forms with equal frequency. Alun Cilie uses the classical syllabic forms in 60% of his compositions, the popular accentuated forms 40%. Dic Jones, the youngest of the poets, uses the syllabic forms in 90% of the poems in *Caneuon Cynhaeaf*. These figures illustrate a growth in the use of the strict forms as the 20th century progresses. This might also be interpreted as a decline in Wales, as elsewhere, in the use of accentuated forms, popular in the 19th century in English and German, for example. A count of the sonnets in *Caniadau Isgarn, Cerddi Alun Cilie* and *Caneuon Cynhaeaf* yields the numbers three, eight, and two respectively. This count accurately represents the sonnet as a healthy by-form in the corpus.

Significantly, in the three volumes chosen to illustrate the frequency with which classical syllabic and popular accentuated metres occur, there are no examples whatsoever of free verse. To find regular use of free verse in the work of the Ceredigion poets, one must look first to the work of J.M. Edwards. In *Ar Awr Ddigalon* (*In a Moment of Despair*), written sometime between 1936 and 1955, Edwards writes, without rhyme in the original, 'On the face of the moon I see blood, and the stars flicker, their eyes filled with fear'. The second poet to depart from rhyme and metre is W.J. Gruffydd in his monumental *Ffenestri* (1961), a work now largely forgotten in Wales.

In the work of John Roderick Rees, we observe free verse vying to oust the older rhyming forms used by the poet, a struggle that marks his work. In total John Roderick Rees published some 200 poems. In the first volume, *Cerddi* (*Poems*) (1984), a volume that includes the contents of *Cerddi'r Ymylon* (*Poems from the Periphery*, 1959), there are 12 sonnets. In *Cerddi Newydd* (*New Poems*) (1992), there are no sonnets. In *Cerddi* there are six *cywyddau*. In *Cerddi Newydd* there are none. In *Cerddi* there are some 25 *englyn*. In *Cerddi Newydd* there are 8 *englyn*. In the book *Cerddi*, other than in *Ffynhonnau* (*Sources*), all texts rhyme. In *Cerddi Newydd* (1992) however, a third of the work is without rhyme, a sign that free verse has finally found a foothold, late in the 20th century.

Our period, however, is much less marked by the advent of free verse than by the rebirth of classical Welsh. During the first half of the 20th century, scholars such as Ifor Williams, Henry Lewis and John Morris Jones laboured to edit and publish Welsh poetry of the classical age, and collections of work by the medieval bards gave currency for the first time in the modern world to work from the 14th to 16th centuries. In 1952, Thomas Parry published *Gwaith Dafydd ap Gwilym* (*The Work of Dafydd ap Gwilym*), a major contribution to Welsh learning. The rural poets of Ceredigion, frequenting, as many of them did, extra-mural classes and *Eisteddfodau*, were acquainted with these standard works, and were well equipped to express their own experiences with increasing sophistication and confidence.

CERDDI
PENTALAR
Ail gyfrol o gerddi
ALUN CILIE
Golygydd
T. LLEW JONES

Jeremiah Jones and the Making of the Tradition

Whatever conditions may be met, or however fertile the ground may be, a tradition will not emerge without the passion and genius of a small number of individuals who impart vision, and whose lives become an inspiration for others. Jeremiah Jones (1855–1902) was one such individual. Who was Jeremiah Jones?

In the year 1886, *The Allotments and Small Holdings Association* published a pamphlet by Frederic Impey entitled '*Three Acres and a Cow, Successful Small Holdings and Peasant Proprietors*', with a foreword by J. Chamberlain, minister in William Gladstone's cabinet of the day. The goals of the society are listed at the beginning of the pamphlet. Among them features the following: 'Generally to facilitate by all legitimate methods the restoration of the rural population to direct connection with the soil'.

This and other developments were a source of jubilation for many labourers and crofters in Britain in the 1880s. Ballads composed in English rang to the chorus of '*Three Acres and a Cow*'. In Wales, in Ceredigion, a similar ballad was composed in the Welsh language by Jeremiah Jones entitled *Tair Erw a Buwch* (*Three Acres and a Cow*). I take the text from *Hen Ŷd y Wlad* (Salt of the Earth) (pp 15-18) by Isfoel:

> 'Chamberlain too is there, old friend to the poor man,
> Standing amidst the Tories and their derision,
> And there he argues our case shrewdly,
> Three acres for the worker and a cow to provide milk,
> Three acres and a cow, three acres and a cow,
> The land to the people, three acres and a cow.'

On April 9th 1855, Jeremiah Jones was born at the old forge, Pen-y-Bryn, near Cilgerran in North Pembrokeshire between the River Teifi and the Preseli Mountains. He followed in his fathers' footsteps, and opened a forge of his own in Goodwick, North Pembrokeshire. In 1876 he married Mary George, and the couple moved to Blaencelyn, just north of Cardigan town. From there, in 1889, he moved with a young and growing family to Cilie Farm, a large holding comprising 300 acres. Jeremiah Jones contracted diabetes in 1896, and died before his 47th birthday in 1902, leaving a widow and a family of twelve to fend for themselves.

Jeremiah Jones' roots can be traced back to a place called Cwm Du in the parish of Brongwyn, near Newcastle Emlyn in Ceredigion. In the 18th century, Cwm Du was home to the bards of the Tomos family who, in their day, carried the old bardic flame. With the collapse of the bardic order in the 16th century during the reign of the Tudors, the custodians of strict metre and classical verse had found themselves patronless, and their tradition then retreated from hall and castle into more modest abodes, where its fire smouldered until fanned to life centuries later under the auspices of the *Eisteddfod*.

A poem by Dic Jones in *Ysgubo'r Storws* (*Sweeping the Storehouse*) entitled *'Y Cilie'* records in verse the legacy of Jeremiah Jones. 'Y Cilie' is the name of the farm where the blacksmith and his family lived after 1889. A sub-heading under the title of the poem reads: 'Blacksmith, Farmer, Poet', part of the inscription on the grave of Jeremiah Jones. The poem tells how the blacksmith came to fan the bardic fire once more, how the quick sparks flew from his anvil, both literally and metaphorically, and how iron was joined to iron in the tradition practiced by his unerring hands. The blacksmith, we are told, wept over the destiny of man, but was moved too to joyous laughter by the wonders of language. His song and art became inseparable, just as Cilie farm and Wales are one and inseparable. In the joys and grief of both the microcosm and the macrocosm, claims Dic Jones, all things the world has ever known may be found, in one form or another.

Tracing the history of the local *Eisteddfodau,* Isfoel writes in *Ail Gerddi Isfoel* (p. 23): 'From the earliest days, the *eisteddfodau* proved infectious for my brothers and me, practically from when the first competitive meetings were held in these parts. The Rev. J. Hawen Rees has told me that he and my father [Jeremiah Jones] formed part of the first committee to organise a [literary] competition in the area. That would have been about the year 1886.' Isfoel also writes: 'My father was one of the most romantic characters ever to have graced the region. He demanded fair play for himself and for all others, and exercised no compromise when dealing with the unjust. He was a poet, a singer, a man of letters ... He instigated competitive [literary] meetings in the area ...' (ibid p. 9)

During his career, Dic Jones dedicates several poems to Jeremiah Jones' youngest son Alun Cilie. There is a light-hearted greeting for his seventieth birthday called *Alun yn Ddeg a Thrigain* (Alun's Seventieth Birthday) (*Caneuon Cynhaeaf*), and two poems in *Storom Awst* to mark the passing of his friend and mentor, one called *Englynion Coffa Alun Cilie* (*Verses in Memory of Alun Cilie*), and the second from which we quote *Yn Angladd Alun* (*At Alun's Funeral*). These texts are commented on in Part IV of *Pen and Plough,* in a chapter dedicated to Dic Jones, *The Final Flourish of the Tradition.*

Alun Cilie passed away in 1975, and for Dic Jones, the tragic and untimely death eight years later in 1983 of Tydfor Jones, a nephew of Alun's, heralds the end of the Cilie era.

This he states clearly in his autobiography: '[It was] another death that shook the region, but one that brought the whole saga of the Cilie Brothers to a close, a saga that had begun a century earlier when Jeremiah Jones, his [i.e. Tydfor's] grandfather settled in Blaencelyn forge... And with his death, it all ended. Now it is no more than a memory' (*Os Hoffech Wybod* pp 266-267). Nevertheless, the legacy of Jeremiah Jones, and of the 18th century bards of Cwm Du, Newcastle Emlyn, lives on in Wales today, in the talent of several branches of the family in Ceredigion, and beyond.

GOMER
T Llew Jones
FY MHOBOL I

The Politics of Poetics

In the work of the rural poets of Ceredigion in the 20th century, there is, on the one hand, writing that is an extension of the Welsh bardic tradition, and, on the other, writing that may be described as British poetry written in Welsh. The latter genre, British poetry, is common in Wales in the 20th century. This distinction is far from watertight, but by using it, much as a one-inch map whose objective is not to provide fine detail, our orientation in the cultural landscape is much the better.

The poets who were born in the 19th century, Isfoel, Evan Jenkins, Isgarn, B.T. Hopkins and Alun Cilie, reached adulthood during the first quarter of the 20th century, and their writing and thinking is informed by native Welsh culture and tradition, rather than by British culture. The work of those born after 1900 tends to fall into two halves. In the latter half of the careers of these poets, the themes of change and loss become ever more resonant. Amongst the relevant changes, attributable to the expansion of English, the British patriotism aroused by two World Wars, and the national image nurtured by radio, television and print media, we note the increasingly British character of Welsh culture as the century unfolds. This state of affairs leads to a strong reaction in the third half of the century, when the nationalist period begins.

T. Llew Jones in his preface to the work of Evan Jenkins Ffair Rhos (1959) writes as follows of another distinction: 'It has been fashionable in Wales for some years now to divide Welsh poets into college bards and country bards, and some may ask to which category Evan Jenkins belongs. This is a difficult question, because given that he is a university graduate, it could be said that he is a college bard.

But I believe he wished to be considered a country bard by all, considering he wrote above all for the rural community in Ceredigion'.

A good example of this debate, academic and rural, literary and oral, Welsh and British, may be found in the introduction to the work of Tregaron shepherd Isgarn, written by T.H. Parry Williams who, after a time in Germany, settled in Aberystwyth as professor of Welsh. Parry-Williams was considered an expert on the folk poetry, and edited of *Hen Benillion,* a scholarly edition of anonymous popular verse from the 18th century. He writes: 'The question has been asked: is it possible for common people to produce verse of any consequence? Can we say that so-called oral literature, never destined to be committed to writing, was the folk equivalent of poetry, whatever meaning we give to the word 'folk'?'

Parry Williams then expands on this question, admitting the emotional and lyrical worth of some of the work of uneducated people, before asking the rhetorical question: 'Was all this not just a simple accident, not the consequence of detailed training or of a thorough knowledge of their craft?' He continues: 'What then is a folk poet? If the term is somewhat derogatory, can a folk poet, through constant practice and by acquiring a measure of culture, develop into something beyond his calling?'

The tone and content of T.H. Parry-Williams' introduction is an excellent instance of the colonisation of the Welsh mind. Wales in the 20th century retains its language, but through this very language, its culture and traditions are infiltrated by the intellectual world that the young Welsh are exposed too in the institutions of higher education which they attend, often in England. Their education complete, their minds opened, but paradoxically, closed, they return to Wales, and apply imported criteria to the culture they were born of but cannot re-embrace fully.

The antithesis to Parry-Williams' confused introduction to the work of Isgarn may be found in an introduction to Isfoel's second volume of poems. Three pages long, and written by Margaret Jenkins, a local woman, the writing is lucid and demonstrates a magisterial understanding of the subject. She writes: 'Today [1965], many people ask, most often in contempt, what we mean by 'the Welsh way of life'. If called on to answer this question, I would refer the inquirer to this book [*Ail Gerddi Isfoel*] and ask where else in Britain can we find this particular type of society that can produce characters like Isfoel?' Margaret Jenkins then returns to the term *bardd gwlad,* folk poet: 'The 'folk poet' has been the object of much reproval, and the term has been much used to cast aspersion on a particular type of poet.' Then, in the following lines, a culture is crystallised by Margaret Jenkins: 'The artist is someone who produces artefacts, whether shaping a blade for a scythe, chiselling a wooden spoon, shaping a pair of horse-shoes, working wood to make a corner cupboard or a fine dresser, or indeed composing *englyn, cywydd* or song.'

Margaret Jenkins then explains the role of the bard in Welsh society: 'The folk poet is the voice of Welsh society, and without him would be much the poorer. When the folk poet has disappeared from Wales, we might as well turn out the lights, because it will be proof that there is no longer life or force enough here to take inspiration from the soil, scatter a handful of seeds, and see it blossom on hill and hedgerow'.

In his book *Teulu'r Cilie* (*The Cilie Family*), Jon Meirion Jones quotes a review of Alun Cilie's first book (1964), by Saunders Lewis, published in *The Western Mail*: 'If you publish poetry today in any of the major languages of

Europe or in any of the European-derived languages of America, you are implicitly laying claim to genius...it is an act of immense self-assertion...But there still exists in Wales another breed, an older breed. These are the heirs of Taliesin, of the court poets of Llywelyn the Great, of the country house poets of the 15th century. We have a name for these poets of aristocracy today; we called them '*beirdd gwlad*' ['folk poets'].'

In these lines, Saunders Lewis shows that the rural poetry of Wales needs to be considered in a broad historical context to be appreciated. Having established this context, he continues with specific reference to Alun Cilie: 'Alun Jones is a master craftsman. First in language...His Welsh is not a glove he puts on. It is the skin of his mind...This '*bardd gwlad*' is disarmingly unassuming. No tragic attitude: no apocalypse. Only the human note and a Greek acceptance.'

Reference to the world of the Greeks is not misplaced. Whereas Christianity introduces the idea of free will, a revolutionary idea in the classical world, pre-Christian civilisations tend to be tied to destiny. The folk poet in Wales, a European peasant, accepts his destiny as custodian of the soil, and does not rebel against what might be perceived as the injustice of the plough in the 20th century, a time when the idea of liberating man from toil finds favour in discourse.

Pausing to consider further some of the ideas in the words of Saunders Lewis, it might be said that the older poets in our corpus have a foot in the medieval world. On occasion, Isfoel's work is unconcerned with sophistication. However, in two *cywydd* of particular note, *Gwynt y Dwyrain* (*The East Wind*) (*Ail Gerddi Isfoel*, p. 67), and *Diolch am Eog* (*Thanks for a Salmon*) (*Ail Gerddi Isfoel*, p. 29), his craft reaches the same heights as the masters of the 14th and 15th century. The subtleties of these compositions are impossible to convey in translation. Suffice to say however, that if judged according to the ideas in T.H. Parry-Williams' introduction to Isgarn, Dafydd ap Gwilym, widely considered a major European poet of the medieval age, would be relegated to the rank of an illiterate village rhymer.

In Welsh, two terms that distinguish between types of verse-making are *prydyddiaeth* or *verse-making,* and *barddoniaeth* or *poetry*. In his autobiography, Dic Jones comments on these terms (p. 131): I know that I am a verse-maker. It is not my place to say whether I am a poet. I do not know where exactly the boundary between the two lies'.

The answer may lie in part in the role of each, poetry and verse-making, *barddoniaeth* and *prydyddiaeth,* in its own specific context. The verse-maker is concerned with entertaining or informing his audience, and his texts and ballads are informed by the events of the day. A popular figure, he stands at the centre of his community. The poet, on the other hand, must often stand at a distance from his fellow man. His motivation is not the entertainment of a given audience, though this may become a consequence of his writing. His role is to challenge, question, and redefine the world. The events of the day will be of less importance to him than to the balladeer and verse-maker, but his career will follow the ebb and flow of ideas in the century in which he lives and writes. In the work of the rural poets of Ceredigion in the 20th century, challenging, questioning and redefining do not amount to a priority. To consider this a weakness would be, however, to misunderstand its function. A tradition, and the merits of a tradition, must be appreciated on their own terms.

CERDDI
Y PREN GWYN
IFAN JONES
Cymdeithas Lyfrau Ceredigion Gyf. Aberystwyth

Bards and Craftsmen

In the 19th century in Wales, and in earlier centuries, rural culture is characterised by the work of the craftsman. Blacksmith, carpenter, clog-maker, tailor, wood-turner, weaver, crofter, tanner and potter: each worked with the medium he was given, whether steel, wood, wool, clay, leather or plough. Each contributed his artefacts to the functioning of the community in which he lived in a relationship of interdependence with his fellows. The bard identified with this community of craftsmen, and the words of the Welsh language were his wood, steel and clay.

The poem *Yr Eingion* (*The Anvil*) by Dic Jones illustrates this. In the collection *Storom Awst* (*August Storm*), the farmer from Aberporth asks how many songs, stories, and rhymes were measured out to the repeated ring of the blacksmith's tap-tap-tap. The comparison between bard and smith is then made loud and clear. From to time to time the poet happens to strike a blow of his own, straightening the point of a nail, while the mallet sets the dance in motion.

In his book *Y Crefftwr yng Nghymru* (*The Craftsman in Wales*) (Gwasg Aberystwyth, 1933), Welsh ethnographer Iorwerth Peate writes (p. 2): 'If an implement made of wood or iron was needed, a plough for what little land there was, or a hook to hang cauldron or kettle on, this implement would be fashioned by the man of the house or by one of the neighbours. Each piece of furniture came from the local workshops, and every stitch of clothing was made from the wool of the sheep that grazed the bare heaths. And in a society such as this it was natural that appreciation should grow of the skill of the craftsman, and of the excellence and capacity of the ordinary man to fashion and create the things needed for everyday life.'

The work done by the craftsman was confined to a designated space. The *tyddynwr* – crofter, small-holder – laboured in the open air. Others had their workshop, the blacksmith his forge, and the various workshops in a village or parish formed a social and cultural network. In *Atgofion Dau Grefftwr* (*Two Craftsmen Remember*), tailor Dan Davies writes: 'In Rhydlewis, as in other villages in South Ceredigion during the first quarter of this [the 20th] century, culture and entertainment was home-spun. There were various craftsmen here, and each had his workshop. To these senates many came to discuss the affairs of the day, and to put the world in its place.'

This world continued to function during the second quarter of the 20th century, but declined during the third quarter, and expired during the fourth. Today in West Wales, the trained eye can pick out old craftsmen's workshops in and around many villages, though most have fallen into disrepair or disappeared. These developments are reflected in the work of the bards and poets of rural Ceredigion. The second poem in Dic Jones' first collection *Agor Grwn* (*Opening a Ridge*) is entitled *Hen Weithdy'r Saer* (*The Carpenter's Old Workshop*). First the scene is described; the door that lies buried under knotted briars, the rust busily consuming the old steel implements. Once a place of excellence, sadness reigns in the workshop now. In *The Carpenter's Old Workshop,* the relationship between craft and bardic practice is reiterated. The carpenter wielded the hammer while nailing a bench, but was also wont to spin verse while carving the wood.

In the collection *Yr Arloeswr* (*The Pioneer*), Dafydd Jones of Ffair Rhos also visits the theme of the craftsman. He makes allusion to carpenter, cobbler, stone-mason and blacksmith in a text six times six lines long that is a concise catalogue of village craftsmen. Written in classical metre, and inspired by folk culture, the poem is a perfect illustration of the world of the rural bard in 20th century Wales. The lines gleam with quiet humour in the original, though in English the tension of the Welsh heptasyllabic line cannot be conveyed. The craftsman, writes Dafydd Jones, is an honest man, hard-working and devoted to his various skills. His craft is a demonstration of precision that he expresses with his fine instruments. The aches and pains that are part of his world, these too he cherishes. And he grows in stature thanks to his difficult task.

There are four poems in Alun Cilie's books that speak of the craftsman: *Hen Fwthyn Deio'r Crydd* (*The Old Workshop of Deio the Cobbler*), *Y Gweithdy* (*The Workshop*), *Y Gof* (*The Blacksmith*), and *Y Saer Maen* (*The Stone-Mason*). The first begins with a reference to the location of the workshop, a toponym evocative of meadow and stream that serves to create the atmosphere of the opening lines. The place is called Dôl Nant, and many summers have passed since the last remnants of its beauty collapsed. Today, writes the poet, it is no more than a crumbling mound. In *The Workshop,* in memory of a certain Siencyn Griffiths, the scene is similar, though in this instance we are afforded a glimpse of the inside of the disused old building. Seeing the place triggers a memory of smell in the poet's mind, the smell of leather. By now however, the valley has fallen into a deep silence, and the skill and know-how of the tanner have been lost.

The Blacksmith and *The Stone-Mason* are a pair of sonnets from Alun Cilie's second book. The first couplet in *The Blacksmith* tells us that thoroughness was the motto of Siôn the blacksmith. To this motto he was true, his whole life long, no matter what was required of him. In the second sonnet, *The Stone-Mason* is described graphically as a man dressed in corduroy trousers, the dawn glowing on his cheek. He wears a waistcoat and hob-nailed boots, smokes a pipe, and is master of the secrets of chiselling and binding stone.

Of the many collections of poetry published by Ceredigion bards in the 20th century, none offer a fuller and more vivid picture than *Y Pentref* (*The Village*) by J. M. Edwards in *Cerddi Hamdden* (*Poems of Recreation*). This text was written as a radio script from the BBC, the first in a series of *pryddestau radio* or long poems for radio. Published in 1962, the text harks back to the village of Llanrhystud in central Ceredigion in the first quarter of the 20th century. The clog-maker speaks, saying that here in the workshop he learned his father's craft. At one time, he says, the wonders he could perform with his hands were held in esteem throughout the land. The ploughman says he could wish for no other life, and desires nothing other than to hold a plough by both shafts, and to see its bright blade slice the furrow. J.M. Edwards writes of others, weavers and stone-cutters, for example. There are also gardeners, men who trained the hedgerows, none of whom went to college, but all of whom are graduates of the countryside.

The reference to education here owes nothing to hazard. Tradition taught the people how to live, but learning was not an institutional affair, and whereas in medieval times the bard sang in hall and castle, in modern times, until the growth of industry changed the world, he sang in the smithies and in the humble workshops of villages such as Rhydlewis and Llanrhystud.

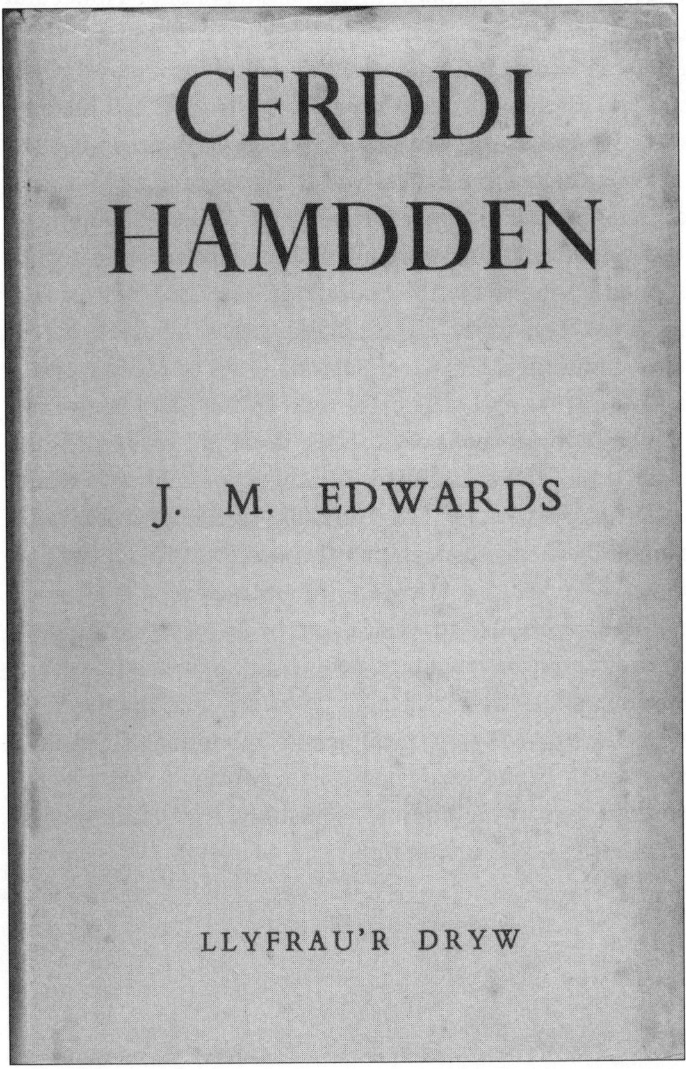
CERDDI
HAMDDEN
J. M. EDWARDS
LLYFRAU'R DRYW

Four Views of the Rural Space

A reading of European poetry from romantic to modern enables us to discern clearly four views of the rural space, *la campagne* in French, and *cefn gwlad* in Welsh. The first view is that of the native metropolitan poet for whom the rural space is distant and alien to varying degrees. The second is of the metropolitan poet who migrates to the rural space, spends some time there, enjoys inspiration there, but remains a stranger to the human society there. The third view of the rural space in the lyric traditions of Europe, from romantic to modern, is that of the rural poet who migrates to the metropole and writes there of his native place as he remembers it, or choses to remember it. And the fourth view, somewhat rarer, is the view of the rural poet who remains in his native environment and writes of the experience of living there.

The first view, that of the native metropolitan for whom the rural space is distant, may be represented by a simple quote from *Les Mots* (1964), an autobiography by Jean-Paul Sartre: 'I have never scratched the earth nor searched for nests, never collected and studied plants, never thrown stones at birds. But books have been my birds and nests, my domesticated animals, my stable and countryside.' Here, indirectly, Sartre, acknowledges the importance of the rural space in French culture. His statement then continues, in tones apologetic, to underline the distance between the rural world and his own, before resolving the tension between the two poles by deriving a metaphor for his life and work from the very milieu, *la campagne,* that he admits is alien to him.

Sartre's point of view typifies the Parisian hegemony in French intellectual life since the earliest modern times until our own day. Within Europe, this metropolitan hegemony is particularly virulent in France, but modern literature and art in Europe in general is typified by a strong association with the major metropoles, and with the cultural and academic institutions that form part of the life of these metropoles. British writers over time have invariably found it imperative to gravitate towards London, if only in the hope of entering circles of influence, and finding a publisher, while in Ireland in the 20th century, few writers of note resisted the lure of the capital city Dublin.

In the German-speaking world, Berlin and Vienna exert their influence: in the latter after World War Two, the Gruppe 47 grows up around Hans Werner Richter, attracting amongst others Ingeborg Bachmann and Paul Celan, while in Romania Eugene Ionescu, Mircea Eliade, Emil Cioran are amongst those who congregate in Bucarest in the early 1930s. In the inter-war period in Poland, the Skamander group of writers were based in Warsaw and retired to Zakopany annually to take the air. The rural space as a result of this centralisation of intellectual activity becomes distant, and peripheral, and the people living there tend to appear in books and paintings in various marginal and stylised ways.

The second view of the rural space in the lyric traditions of Europe is that of the metropolitan poet who migrates to the rural space, spends some time there, enjoys inspiration there, but remains a stranger, in part or in full, to human society there. This view characterises the romantic movement in general, and is a view that informs some of the work of Gerard Manley Hopkins (1844–1889) and certain poems by William Wordsworth (1770–1850). Hopkins spent several years in the Clwyd Valley, North-East Wales, between earlier periods in London and industrial Lancaster, and a later period in Dublin, where he died. In *Hurrahing in the Harvest*, Hopkins writes:

> 'Summer ends now; now, barbarous in beauty, the stooks arise Around; up above, what wind-walks! What lovely behaviour Of silk-sack clouds!'

Another poem by Hopkins is *The Sea and the Skylark*. In this poem, Hopkins finds himself by the sea by the town of Rhyl where he hears the lark sing rapturously. He considers the beauty of sea and lark, and then compares them to the town:

> 'How these two shame this shallow and frail town!
> How ring right out our sordid turbid time...'

Turning to Wordsworth's *Tintern Abbey*, there is the following reference, similar in tone to that of Hopkins, to the urban milieu:

> 'These beauteous forms,
> Through a long absence, have not been to me
> As is a landscape to a blind man's eye:
> But oft, in lonely rooms, and 'mid the din
> Of towns and cities, I have owed to them
> In hours of weariness, sensations sweet.'

Wordsworth in *Tintern Abbey* makes reference in the following terms to human inhabitation of the rural space he visits:

> 'Once again I see these hedge-rows, hardly hedge-rows,
> Little lines of sportive wood run wild: these pastoral farms,
> Green to the very door, and wreaths of smoke
> Sent up, in silence, from among the trees.'

This human world is one he does not engage with here however. Its people in this instance remain faceless. From the rural space as depicted above by both poets, the people who inhabit the space are absent. There is no investigation of the human culture to which the rural space is home. 'The stooks arise around,' writes Hopkins in *Hurrahing in the Harvest*. He tells nothing of the hands that built the stooks. 'The things were here and but the beholder wanting'. The harvesters too were present to behold the wonders of creation. Of them however we are told nothing.

In the rural space, the romantic poet will find manifestations not of humanity but of divinity. Subsequently, the space begins to assume degrees of symbolism. It becomes a space that has been moved from, a space to be returned to, but a space that is presumed to have remain unchanged during one's absences from it. It becomes a retreat from the urban world and thus develops into an antithesis of this world. Part of this antithesis is the perceived fact of the rural space being unpeopled.

The third view of the rural space is the view of the poet issue of a rural environment who migrates away from his home place towards an urban or metropolitan world. In European poetry, this view is represented particularly well in Ireland, a country that remained largely unindustrialised deep into the 20th century. We look first at *The Great Hunger*, a long poem by Patrick Kavanagh (1904–1967) published in 1947.

The poem is typical in certain ways of much of the poetry written in Ireland by poets born in the first half of the twentieth century. Ireland at this time was an underdeveloped country suffering in several ways from its colonial past. Its economy was weak, its infrastructure skeletal, its society stagnant, its people disillusioned and ripe for emigration. Those who remained at home to farm the land battled with depression, sexual frustration, and with the realisation that their prospects were extremely limited. This is the type of society from which Irish writers looked to free themselves through education and a career in an urban environment, most often in the capital city Dublin. Kavanagh's *The Great Hunger,* a text some five thousand words long, captures the atmosphere of mid-twentieth century rural Ireland:

> 'Poor Paddy Maguire, a fourteen-hour day
> He worked for years.....
> His mother tall hard as a Protestant spire
> Came down the stairs barefoot at kettle-call
> And talked to her son sharply:
> 'Did you let the hens out, you?'

These lines Kavanagh wrote after moving away from his native Monaghan. The writing illustrates his intimate acquaintance with the rural world he describes, but in the poem the author distances himself from it. Thus, at the beginning of the poem, in line 4, he establishes a clear distinction between those within, 'Maguire and his men, and those without, referred to simply as 'we':

> 'Clay is the word and clay is the flesh
> Where the potato-gatherers like mechanised scarecrows move
> Along the side-fall of the hill – Maguire and his men.
> If we watch them an hour is there anything we can prove
> Of life...?'

In the work of Hopkins and Wordsworth, the reader meets men who find manifestations of divinity in the rural space, whereas in the work of Kavanagh we encounter a man who finds manifestations of mortality there:

> 'Patrick Maguire, the old peasant, can neither be damned nor glorified:
> The graveyard in which he will lie will be just a deep-drilled potato-field
> Where the seed gets no chance to come through...'

The fourth view of the rural space in European poetry from romantic to modern is the view of the rural poet who remains in his native environment and writes of the experience of living there. This view is represented best on the peripheries of the continental space, in Romania in the east, and in Wales in the west. Romanian poet and philosopher Lucian Blaga derives his work from manifestations of life in the rural space. Here first is an excerpt from the poem *Sufletul Satului* (*Spirit of a Country Place*):

> It seems to me that eternity was born into a country place
> All thought seems slower there
> Slower too the beating of the heart
> As though the breast were not its source
> But a place deeper within the earth.

In Wales, in Ceredigion, J.R. Jones of Tal-y-bont, Dafydd Jones of Ffair Rhos, Isgarn of Blaencaron, B.T. Hopkins of Y Mynydd Bach, John Roderick Rees of Bethania, the Cilie brothers Alun and Dafydd (Isfoel) of Cwmtydu, and Dic Jones of Aberporth all belong to a school of poets who remain in their native rural environment and write of the experience of living there. Unlike their metropolitan colleagues, unlike the romantic wanderers, these poets are not outsiders in the rural space, observing a landscape and deriving aesthetic pleasure or inspiration from it without engaging with human society there. On the contrary, they speak on behalf of the people, and their work is a testimony to the people, their endeavours, their joys and tribulations. In the following chapters, we enter the world of these bards, poets, farmers, ploughmen and shepherds, see the faces of the people, and hear the voices of a culture hitherto unknown outside Welsh-speaking Wales.

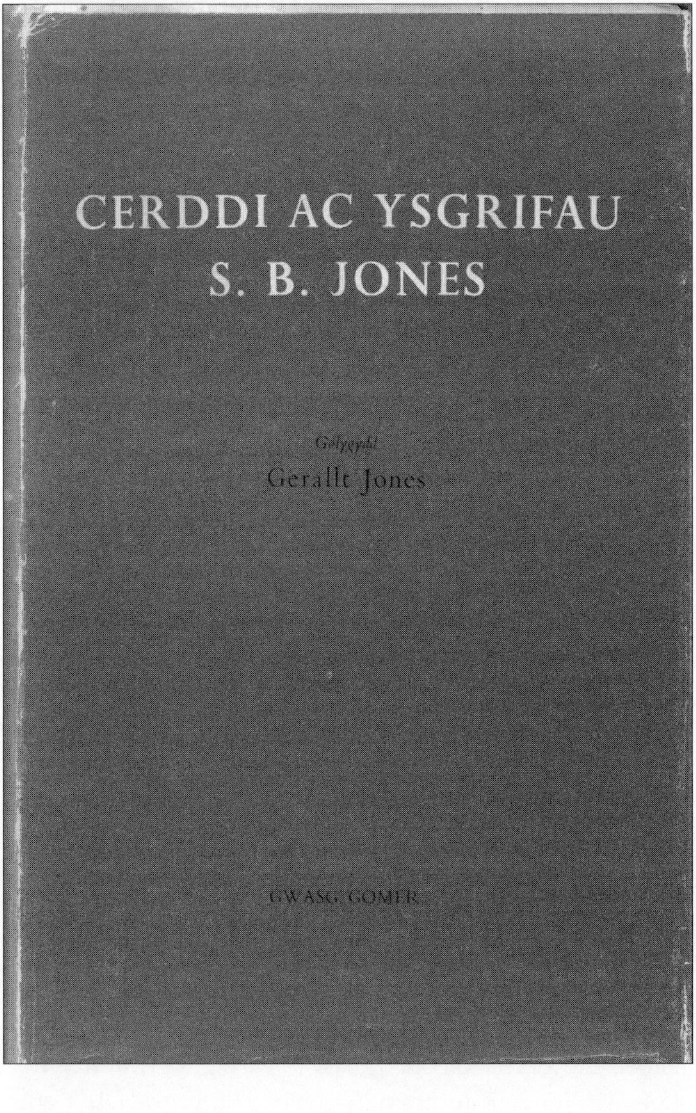
CERDDI AC YSGRIFAU
S. B. JONES
Golygydd
Gerallt Jones
GWASG GOMER

PART II

THE LAND

Landlord and Tenant

After the First World War, the day of tenant and landlord recedes into the past, and there are few references to what had become a bygone age. In his autobiography, *Os Hoffech Wybod* (*Should You Care to Know*), Dic Jones writes as follows (p.152): 'The old estates were dismantled, and many farmers who had formerly been tenants in them then bought their own places from these estates'. By our period, the 20th century, the landlord has all but disappeared, and the tenant becomes proprietor. Looking closely at the poems however, footprints on overgrown paths are still there to be found.

The nineteenth century in Ceredigion, as in Britain and Ireland in general, was a time of aristocratic power when the poor feared hunger and eviction, and from 1874 until 1880, while in government, the Tories incurred the wrath of small farmers nationwide owing to their treatment of the question of land ownership. In his famous ballad of 1886, *Tair Erw a Buwch* (*Three Acres and a Cow*), blacksmith Jeremiah Jones wrote as follows:

> 'Down with landlordism, the oppression of our time
> Along with stewardship, unjust and immoral;
> Down with the idler, let the worker prevail
> The land for the people, three acres and a cow.'

Isfoel, the oldest of our poets, born in 1881, and son of Jeremiah Jones, is author of *Hen Blas y Bronwydd* (*Ail Gerddi*

Isfoel pp. 36-38), the only text in the corpus dedicated in its entirety to the subject of the landlord. The poem, a historical ballad in the popular style, describes the demise of the manor house and the end of its influence in south Ceredigion. In it, we meet a beggar, grey-faced, head bent, who comes to the back door of the manor overcome with fatigue. The reference to the man seeking alms suggests that vagrancy was not uncommon at the time. The lady of the house is presented as a kind and charitable mistress.

Isfoel's text also depicts the lord of Bronwydd House in a favourable light, stating that Sir Martin and his forebears were patrons in former times of a tradition which they upheld and cultivated. Isfoel describes the landlord as a father figure, and as a king to the tenants of the estate. Then comes evidence of the social changes of the time. The castle falls and is obliterated. Y Bronwydd, a house of privilege, its architecture so imposing in an area of humble cottages, comes crashing down, and today it is but a mound, the lord in his grave.

Isfoel's fond view of Sir Martin and Lady Lloyd resonates in remarks made by David Jenkins in *The Agricultural Community in South-West Wales* where we read (p. 26): 'The Lloyds, who had long been resident at Bronwydd, were noted for their generosity and for their support of churches and non-conformist chapels in the area'. Various other landlords in Ceredigion were less well respected than the Lloyds of Bronwydd, as we shall see below.

Certain aspects of life during the time of the landlords is described in our corpus by John Roderick Rees and W.J. Gruffydd. Between 1750 and 1860, much land in Britain and Ireland was made subject to a series of acts of enclosure. In *Cau'r Tiroedd Comin* (*Enclosing the Commonage*) (Gwasg y Brython, Liverpool, 1952), David Thomas writes (p. 27):

'In 1795, there were 206,720 acres of commonage in Cardiganshire while by 1895, there remained a mere 33,264 acres'.

This meant that land used by the people as commonage became unavailable to them for grazing, for the collection of wild plants, nuts and fruit. However, some land, including poorer mountain land, did remain unenclosed. For this reason, and others – demographic change for example – some movement towards higher ground occurred in 19th century Wales. Here, a man could claim a certain territory on condition that he build a house in one night, and that smoke rise from the chimney by sun-rise. These *tai unnos* were built in Ceredigion.

> In *Y Winllan* (*The Vineyard*) by John Roderick Rees (*Cerddi John Roderick Rees,* pp 45-50), the poet tells us how, one night by the light of the moon, a man works stealthily, piling stone upon cold stone to build a house for the summer that his kindred could inhabit. His endeavours are repaid, and on the equinox at Michaelmas he crosses the threshold of his mountain hut. Smoke is seen to rise, unfolding into the blue skies, a sign that the work is complete. After the tempestuous exertion of a single short night, the builder of the house then enjoys some respite before rising meet the challenge of life on the bare mountain.
>
> In the long poem *Ffenestri* (*Windows*) (*Ffenestri a Cherddi Eraill,* p. 12), W.J. Gruffydd, also writes of the building of the *tai unnos,* the one-night houses, in the uplands of Ceredigion. He portrays a niche of moorland where, spade and shovel in hand, a courageous man once came to build himself a one-night house before the sun's slender fingers dismissed the stars and pushed the moon into the sea. Only the cruellest heart could deny

him his barren slice of mountain, says the poet. where nothing grows but heather and rushes, and ears of yellow gorse nod their weary heads as the wind pontificates.

In the work of J.R. Jones Tal-y-bont in North Ceredigion between Aberystwyth and The Dyfi Estuary, the landlord appears in several poems, in *Dagrau* ('*Tears*') for example. The poet describes how poverty and hunger scoured the land, and how a foreign landlord feasted thirstily on the hard toil of the small holders.

Yr Hen Blas ('*The Old Manor House*) describes the estate of Hafod Uchtryd near Pont-ar-Fynach in the mountains on the Rheidol river where, in the early 19th century, a man called Thomas Johnes (1748–1816) pioneered modern agriculture for the benefit of all. J.R. Jones evokes the pioneer, and old gentleman, silent now on his cold mausoleum. There are none to remember him, says the poet, only the wild tenant moon who keeps its secrets locked safely away.

The most poignant reference in the poetry of Ceredigion to tyranny against the poor in the 19th century occurs in the poem *Y Pasg* (*Easter*) by J.R. Jones. Here a certain Ifan Huws y Foel, one of a gallery of characters who appear in the poem, remembers a scene from his childhood. He recalls how a foreign bailiff came strutting through the farmyard, spitting his words into the face of his skeletal father who lay, near death, on his poster bed. The bailiff cared nothing for the sweat on the old man's brow, nor for the flecks of blood on the pillow. He gives the sick and elderly tenant a week's grace, threatening to throw him into jail if he fails to pay, but death comes calling first, two days before the bailiff's return.

In *Y Pentref* (*The Village*) by J.M. Edwards, (*Cerddi Hamdden*), a long poem about life in Llanrhystud village early in the 20th century, the farmer makes brief reference to the day of the landlord. These things however are already just a memory. The farmer remembers his father who farmed Tŷ Hen in the village all his life long, and how he sometimes spoke of the tyranny of the landlords, of the grinding toil, and the cross he had to bear.

The final throes of one estate, Tan-y-Bwlch near Aberystwyth in mid-Ceredigion, are described by Caroline Palmer in the *Journal of the Ceredigion Antiquarian Society* (Volume XIV, no. 1, pp 37-78); 'Following his death [i.e. of Vaughan Davies, 'Lord Ystwyth' (1840–1935)], auctioneers John Francis and Son auctioned the Tan-y-Bwlch Estate in 26 lots on 27 July 1936. Vaughan Davies's lands had shrunk by more than 3,000 acres since 1872. The Tan-y-Bwlch estate now consist[ed] of just 678 acres'.

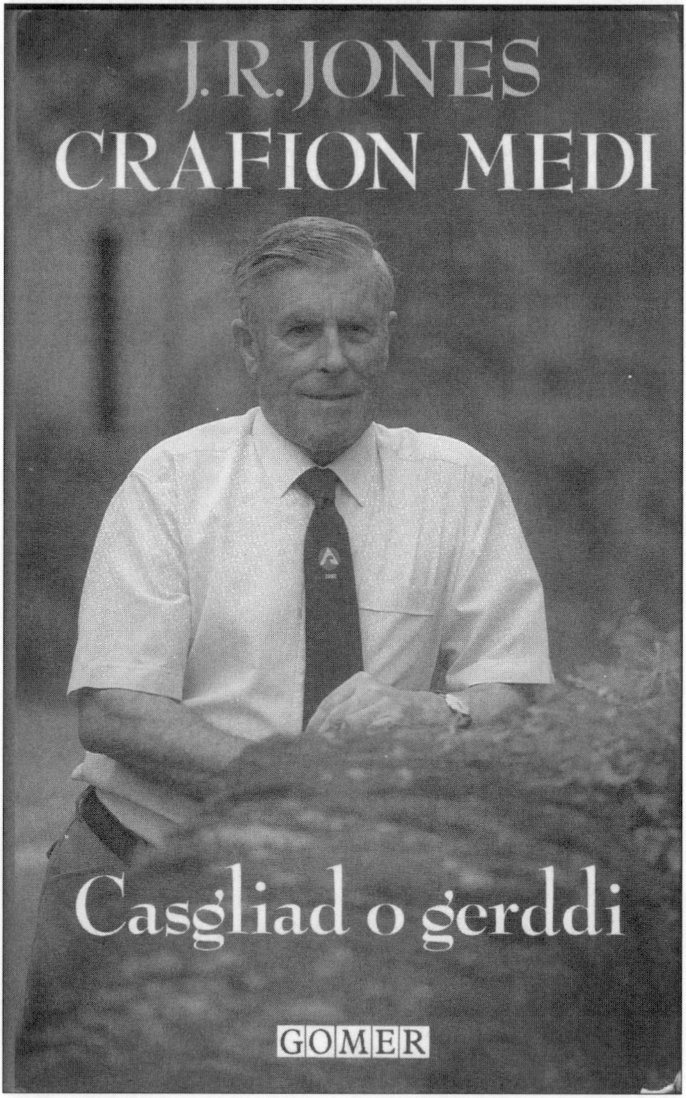
J.R. JONES
CRAFION MEDI
Casgliad o gerddi
GOMER

Utopia and Dystopia

From the 16th century on, a cultural dualism emerged in Wales that enriches the tensions that characterise the country at different times. The Catholic religion was prohibited, as was the case throughout the kingdom. However, in Wales, elements of a culture that had its origins in the pre-Tudor world continued to be practiced: the Welsh still swore on David's bones, *yr asgwrn Dafydd,* and those of other saints, until the end of the 20th century.

Popular superstitions remained strong, not declining but flourishing in early modern times. In *Coelion Cymru* (*The Beliefs of Wales*) Evan Isaac writes at length of *y tylwyth teg* (the little people), presagers of death, predicting the future, spells and charms, the *toili* (a funeral cortege from the other world), and other archaic practices. The following example, a beseeching, is from Llanerfyl, Montgomeryshire, and Isaac dates it to the 'beginning of the 19th century'. We note the reference to 'evil spirits': 'O Lord Jesus Christ I beseech thee to preserve me Edwards Jones, my horses, cows, calves, pigs and sheep and every living creature that I possess from the power of all evil men, women, spirits or wizards...'

In most parts of Wales, until the late 19th century, the annual feast of parish saint, known in Welsh as *Gŵyl Mabsant,* continued to be celebrated with traditional enthusiasm. Games, including early forms of football and hockey, cock-fights, drinking and dancing were all synonymous with the Mabsant festival. The annual festival of the parish saint was not the only time for pleasure. A popular verse from *Hen Benillion,* edited by T.H. Parry Williams, reads as follows (p. 64):

'I went courting one Friday night
Under the barrel in the cellar
I can tell you I would dearly love
To have my way with her again.'

During the 19th century, the culture described above begins to change both in Wales and in Europe. A process of urbanisation begins that causes a departure from older traditions. Folk beliefs gradually become obsolete. In Wales, non-conformism continues to grow, and with it a new moral code. Industrialisation brings about demographic shifts. The cathartic Mabsant festival, comparable to German *Fastnacht* or *Karneval,* to *Mardi gras,* or to the ancient Greek orgy, is abandoned, and outward manifestations of respectability are expected of members of society at all times. The passage from the 19th to the 20th century in Wales also ushers in the question of a new British-Welsh dual identity. In his autobiography (1989), Dic Jones makes the following remark (p. 78): 'Presumed that Napoleon's [sic] description of us British as 'a nation of shop-keepers' is correct...' Here, Dic Jones writes of 'us British' quite naturally. This is consistent with the fact that Welsh people born in the second quarter of the 20th century and later had in general come to consider themselves British.

The effects of the changes outlined above produce a certain trauma, and this is reflected to an extent in the work of some of the Ceredigion poets in the 20th century, T. Llew Jones, Dic Jones and J.M. Edwards, for example.

In *Caethiwed* (*Captivity*), T. Llew Jones describes his heart as a bird trapped in a cage. He hears the furious beating of its wings, and when it senses the wall is closing in, it throws itself at the windows of the cell seeking to free itself. In another poem, *Evan Humphries, Penlôn,* the T. Llew Jones describes his subject as a devout man, but cannot understand why a devout man would tie pagan ribbons to his door to welcome the month of May. The poem tells how, on the eve of May each year, the honest old weaver Evan Humphries would welcome summer after a long winter by adorning his door and window with freshly-cut leaves. In both these instances, the poet admits to being troubled by these contradictions, things he has difficulty in grasping. He stops shorts of pursuing the theme however.

In a very small number of poems, Dic Jones confronts briefly the inner demons that festivals such as Mabsant helped to banish from heart and mind once a year in former times in Wales. Two of these are *Wynebau* (*Faces*) and *Miserere*. In the first, the poet describes his other face, a face even his loved ones have never seen. This, he says, is the face of his failings and greatest fears. When he looks in the mirror, this face troubles him, but he shall not confess it. The malevolence in his other face is not apparent, but he the poet can see it nonetheless. In these lines, Dic Jones closes the door on one part of the mind and soul, the part of darkness, and this door will not be reopened.

In *Miserere,* a poem eight quatrains long, life has lost all appeal for poet Dic Jones. Warm companionship brings him no solace, nor do words of well-meaning friendship. Nobody, he writes, can know the mute suffering of his neighbour. None live in a land that is free of pain. These ideas remain latent, but are not teased out or investigated in the work of Dic Jones, nor in the work of T. Llew Jones.

J.M. Edwards, on the other hand, is perhaps the only poet of his day from West Wales who strives with artistic honesty to come to terms with the meaning of human solitude, of doubt and despair, and of the shadows cast by the chaos of the modern world. In a long and reflective poem, *Bywyd* (*Life*), written between 1924 and 1935, J.M. Edwards speaks of a wild beast constantly sending pagan shudders through his flesh. This beast stirs up the passions of the mud and forest, taking delight in a rational, civilised man's fickle destiny. The beast tears the poet's breast with his sharp claws. Day after day he sows chaos. There is no escape from his influence, from the beast's desire to tear the poet's every limb apart. This terrible psychological ordeal continues, and J.M. Edwards feels suffocating weight of his own natural desires pressing upon him. He asks how in the world he can escape from the relentless weariness that plagues his being, and whether anywhere on earth there is sanctuary from these raging emotions, inherited from the shadowy forests. The answers to J.M. Edwards' question lie, in part at least it seems, in folk cultures discarded by industrial Wales and Europe in the late nineteenth century.

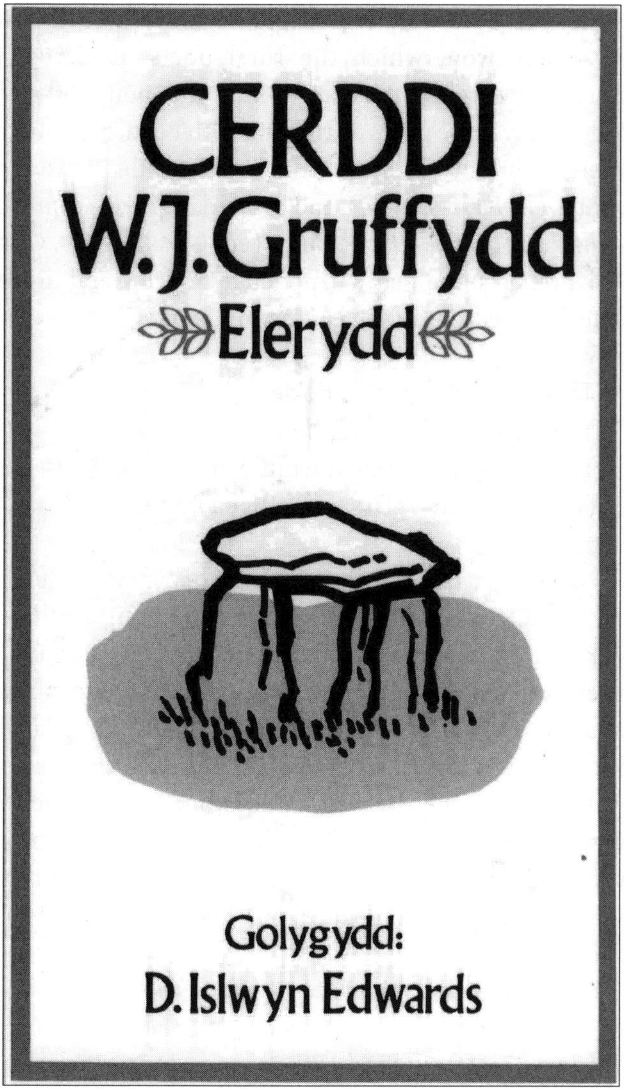
CERDDI
W. J. Gruffydd
Elerydd
Golygydd:
D. Islwyn Edwards

Alcohol and Temperance

The consumption of alcohol in Wales in the late 19th century precedes various developments that are relevant to the society from which the rural poets of Ceredigion emerge, and relevant therefore to the body of poetry produced by these poets during the 20th century. A quatrain by Jeremiah Jones, written about 1886, entitled *Y Gwydraid Cyntaf* (*The First Glassful*), and printed in *Awel Ysgafn y Cilie* (*Light Verse by The Cilie Family*) (ed. Gerallt Jones, Gomer 1976), reflects one man's experience of drink and drinking in the final decades of the century in Ceredigion:

'This is the glass with a tickle
It calls for another, and then:
'Three, five, ten, bring me more' the craving calls,
Yes, this the first glass will father a hundred.'

In a collection of portraits of local characters around the turn of the century *Hen Ŷd y Wlad* (*Salt of the Earth*), the blacksmith's son Isfoel tells an anecdote concerning his father Jeremiah Jones. The expression 'at that time' is revealing of subsequent change: 'Tom and Jeremiah had gone to some auction or other near Penmorfa, and there was plenty of drink there as was the custom at that time.' The anecdote continues to tell how the same 'Tom' fell into the river in Llangrannog, and is one of three drink-related anecdotes that Isfoel includes in the pages devoted to his father.

In the same collection, *Awel Ysgafn y Cilie* (*Light Verse by The Cilie Family*), we find a ballad called *Cwrw Awcsion* (Auction Beer) written in 1898 by Fred Jones, the eldest of the Cilie brothers. The theme was set for a competition in lyric composition at the Glynarthen *Eisteddfod*. At the time, in order to help push prices up at an auction, dealers would offer the punters free beer, an offer difficult to refuse after a thirsty journey by horse and cart, or on foot. In verse six of thirteen Fred Jones writes:

'Beer to make the wares the dearer
Beer to make the eye go blind
Beer to show the false attractions
Of washed out old things of little value.'

In the first couplet in verse ten, he writes of the many who supped on the auctioneer's beer and who today are threadbare and impoverished. In the closing verses of the ballad comes the call for reform than soon echoed loud around the country:

'Children of the evangel in the Land of the Hills
Wake from your slumber wherever you may be,
Be principled when making an offer
And dispel the beer of shame from your midst.'

Two things happened in tandem during the very early years of the 20th century that had a profound change on attitudes towards drink and drinking in Welsh culture. One was the religious revival of 1904–05, the other the blossoming of the temperance movement. In *Gwyddoniadur Cymru* (The Encyclopaedia of Wales) under 'Temperance' we read: 'The first society for abstention [from alcoholic beverages] in Wales was established in Llanfechell [Anglesey] in 1835. A lively abstentionist culture developed, with magazines, meetings, songs, orders, ceremonies, guest-houses and certificates, and by 1850 abstention had become an integral part of the moral fabric of Non-Conformism.' The entry in the *Encyclopaedia* continues: 'In Wales, the greatest success of the movement was the closure of public houses on Sunday, and this was enshrined in Welsh national law in 1881'.

The religious revival of 1904–05 is described by John Davies in *A History of Wales* (p. 505): '...the revival of 1904–5 [was] one of the most extraordinary happenings in twentieth-century Wales. It began in February 1904 in southern Cardiganshire; the 'foster father' of the revival, according to R. Tudur Jones, was the South Cardigan Calvinistic Methodist Monthly Meeting.'

The 1904–05 revival is mentioned occasionally by Ceredigion writers born in the late 19th century. Former miner W. Jones-Edwards devotes a short chapter to the subject in his autobiography *Ar Lethrau Ffair Rhos* (*On the Slopes of Ffair Rhos*). His homely prose puts a very human face on a childhood memory. 'On our way home from the Meeting, Auntie and I would call in Blaenesgair. On the neat old hearth, there sat an old woman we called Mari Blaenesgair. Old age prevented her from attending the prayer meetings she loved so much. Mari was always eager to hear about the meetings, but nothing pleased me more than to see Mari smoking...She was completely toothless, and I loved to see her poking a roll of thin paper into the fire, guiding it with shaking hand to the tip of her [clay] pipe, and drawing on it until her cheeks grew hollow...This was the highlight of the prayer meeting on the mountain for me.'

Of the elderly women who occur in our corpus, not all came under the reforming influence of the Religious Revival of 1904–5. Isgarn states this in *Yr Helfa* (*Gathering*). The poem opens the door on a world that, already in his day, was somewhat archaic. The shepherd is witness to scene that speak perhaps of poverty, but not of indignity. The poem introduces us to a female figure living in seclusion on the mountain, who gathers berries from a pool to be sold for a modest price. Ann Lena is her name, a little old woman, poor and sisterless. One day in late July, the poet sees her go down on her knees in the mountain stream where she is working. This half-pagan image of Ann Lena in the pantheistic wilds has little to do with the iconography that emerged in Wales after 1904–5 and tended, amongst other things, towards portraits of preachers and other influential figures, predominantly male.

The Religious Revival of 1904-05 contributed to bringing about one of the most controversial books of its time in Wales, *My People* by Caradog Evans (David Evans 1878–1945), short story writer and novelist, born in Llanfihangel-ar-Arth, Carmarthenshire. After the untimely death of his father, an auctioneer, his mother and her five children moved to Rhydlewis, Cardiganshire. In 1897 Caradog Evans was apprenticed to a draper in Carmarthen. Later he worked as a shop assistant in Barry, Cardiff and London. While in London he found employment as a journalist in 1906. His first collection of short stories, *My People* (1915), brought him instant notoriety. Two further volumes followed, *Capel Sion* (1916) and *My Neighbours* (1919). Among Caradog Evans' novels were *Morgan Bible* and *Nothing to Pay*.

Caradog Evans' work has direct relevance to the present study of the poetry of the rural poets of Ceredigion in that the two corpuses offer opposing views of the society of the time. Evans' depicts the Welsh Methodists of Southern Ceredigion as bigoted and hypocritical, whilst in the work of local Welsh-language authors, they were, to quote from *A History of Wales* by John Davies again (p. 462), 'cheerful, prudent and godly'.

Central to the bardic community of Southern Ceredigion in the mid-twentieth century was a primary-school teacher named T. Llew Jones who encouraged several local bards to publish their work, and who prefaced many of the volumes of the day. Author of two volumes of verse himself, twice winner of the chair at the National *Eisteddfod,* writer of popular children's books, and an accomplished chess-player, T. Llew Jones promotes the latter image of the rural Welsh society he loved. To an extent, his work is a redressal of the perceived injustice of Caradog Evans' book. Late in his career, T. Llew Jones published a series of essays about local people under the transparent title *Fy Mhobol i* (*My People*). This book contains a five-page chapter entitled *Gelyn y Bobl* (*Enemy of the People*), a reference to Caradog Evans and his work. The following quote from the essay will suffice to illustrate the polarisation of positions regarding *My People* and its author. T. Llew Jones writes (p. 139): 'The evening before Caradog's funeral, his wife, a woman calling herself Countess Barcynska, contacted the late J. R. Evans asking him to hire some local people who would be willing to act as mourners at the funeral. She said she was willing to pay a pound each to any who might come.' The vindictive nature of this anecdote seems, ironically, to suggest that Caradog Evans may have been justified, in part at least, when he published descriptions such as the following (*My People,* Seren, 1987, p. 112): 'There was no movement from Nanni. Mishtir Bryn-Bevan went on his knees and peered at her. Her hands were clasped tightly together, as though guarding some great treasure. The minister raised himself and prised them apart with the ferrule of his walking-stick. A roasted rat revealed itself.'

Nothing could be further from this dystopia than the vision of rural life we find in the verse of T. Llew Jones. In one of few poems in which a Ceredigion poet chooses a subject beyond his native environment, T. Llew Jones writes, in tones almost Aryan, of *Connemara* in the West of

Ireland. In this text from the collection *Sŵn y Malu* (*The Sound of Grinding*), the poet speaks of the Gaelic race who cling to the land in Connemara, men who walk tall, are handsome and endowed with strength, and who believe in God and in his unfailing harvest.

In *A History of Wales* (p. 462), John Davies comments further on life in rural Wales in the early years of the 20th century: 'Between 1900 and 1913, prices of agricultural produce rose by 18%, and in consequence there was a degree of prosperity in the countryside. Later generations were to have an appealing image of Welsh rural society at the turn of the century...Indeed, a great deal of the Welsh literature of the 20th century is an elegy for that golden age'.

In a poem by Alun Cilie, *Yr Hen Gapel* (*The Old Chapel*), we find a reflection of these things. The numbers of chapel-goers swelled during the Revival of 1904–05, and fell off again a decade later. This may help explain why the chapel in Alun Cilie's poem fell into disuse. The text speaks of the old chapel, an eye-sore on the face of the land. The edifice is empty and unlit. The place has become featureless, its complexion is grey, and it is no longer frequented as was once the case. The poet describes it as an abode of saints, and as the Bethlehem of all their hopes. Today however the briar curls over its door, there are brambles in its splendid courtyard, and weeds bar the way all around it. In short, it is little more than an ill-kept dump.

We soon meet the people who worshipped at the old chapel, portrayed by Alun Cilie as being virtuous, a country folk who built a place of worship to honour their Guardian, and a chapel in which to express allegiance to the true God. With bare hands they raised this building that stood proud on a bed of solid rock, and whose grandeur bore testimony to their pride. Even now in times of decay, its structure, its gables and strong arches, testify to their painstaking patience. Times have changed however, and by the mid-20th century the flame has long since died, the coming and going ceased, and pulpit fallen mute. Once the servants of heaven sang there together in swelling voice, but the community now lies at peace in the clay. And from its silence the chapel eyes the desolation, as the world rushes by without pausing to spare it a thought.

In North Ceredigion, in Nant-y-Moch, where in 1964 a reservoir was constructed to supply the Aberystwyth area with electricity, a chapel called Tabor-y-Mynydd is described by J.R. Jones in tones similar to those adopted by Alun Cilie. Tabor-y-Mynydd is in a sorry state, and over the rushy paths the people no longer come by moonlight to communion. The hymns have fallen silent, so too the prayer-meetings, writes J.R. Jones after 1964.

The swelling voices and the hymns that rang ecstatically through the mountains and valleys in 1904–5 and thereafter reach their end in a lonely and poignant poem by John Roderick Rees in his final collection *Cerddi Newydd* (*New Poems*). In *Sul o Ragfyr: Bethania 1987* (*A Sunday in December: Bethania 1987*), the poet writes of 'a congregation big enough to fill only the choir, dotted sparsely over the floor, like a map of an upland population, the demography of the end'.

CERDDI
FFAIR RHOS
Evan Jenkins
Gwasg Aberystwyth

Clearing the Land

In *Cerddi'r Bwthyn* (*Poems from the Cottage*), an allusion to the house in Talgarreg where he spent his twilight years, preacher, soldier and four-times crowned bard Dewi Emrys (1879–1952) dedicates a *cywydd* some seventy lines long to *Y Chwynnwr,* (*The Weeder*). Here, in the rolling proud *cynghanedd* of a master of strict bardic metre, a light is shone on an arduous and inglorious task, that of clearing the land for the seed. Dewi Emrys writes of a man afoot at dawn, valiant in battle, ravager of briar and bramble. Without the work he does, the glory of the harvest would never be. When he has finished his task, the land shall become a garden, and summer's fair hand shall bedeck it in finery.

This is the only poem in the body of work composed in Ceredigion in the 20th century, and perhaps in the Welsh tradition in its entirety, that celebrates at length the primary task of ridding the soil of undesirable growth. Dewi Emrys tells how *The Weeder* removes bushes, relentlessly eliminating sedge, reed, thistle and other unsightly intrusive growth. All these, he says, soon expire and wither. Ultimately, the labour pays good dividends. The earth's cheeks are smoothed, the labourer emerges victorious, and the furrows are a golden wave heavy with grain when summer is in full flood.

In *The Agricultural Community in South-West Wales at the turn of the Twentieth Century,* David Jenkins describes the land and physiography of Ceredigion in a way that lends context to the work of Dewi Emrys's heroic farmer: 'Between the river [Teifi] and the sea stands a ridge, wider and higher to the north-east, narrower and lower towards the south-west where the ridge finally declines into the vale of Teifi. The higher hills are exposed to the sea winds, their soils are acid and peaty, and tree growth is stunted. Where the hill tops are lower the moorland character is less obvious or absent, the soils less acid and of greater depth. But everywhere, at elevations greater than 500 feet, the natural vegetation tends to heath.'

In this passage, David Jenkins identifies characteristics that dictate the development of agriculture in various sub-territories. Life on the mountain is challenging, as we read in the work of the Ffair Rhos poets and of John Roderick Rees. Further south, a more clement environment favours better harvests, this in its turn finding expression in the expansive poetry of Dic Jones, and in the often care-free compositions of others, Isfoel for example, and his brother Alun Cilie.

David Jenkins continues his description of the region as follows: 'Inland from the central ridge of South Cardiganshire run the tributaries of the Teifi. Their valleys are generally narrow, their sides occasionally too deep for horses to plough and the bottoms reed-strewn and boggy. Thus the better farm land is on the extensive intermediary slopes'.

These narrow valleys are typical of the place where *The Weeder* toils in Dewi Emrys' poem, seeking to claim a further acre of arable land from the inhospitable terrain. In *Gelynion* (*Enemies*), Alun Cilie records the trials of a married couple seeking to establish themselves on such terrain. He too makes explicit reference to the task of clearing the land. The small-holder in question is called Wil Yr Hafod, a man whose only reward has long been the sweat of his brow. He wages his sore struggle with the uncultivated land, hewing and chopping, claiming an acre from the wilderness, tending and turning the soil until it yields its fruit. *Enemies,* a poem some one hundred and fifty lines long, is the most detailed and intimate portrait we have of the struggle for survival in the rural space. Fear of poverty, writes the poet, numbs the young couple. The wolf bares its teeth, and the crofter quietly addresses his daunting task. The passion of the early years carries him on, but passion alone cannot sustain him indefinitely. 'Must I spend my life bound to the poverty of this cottage?' he asks despairingly, subject to the whims of the weather, to God's grace, and dependent on neighbourly charity.

The word for charity in the original Welsh text is '*cardod*', a word which has technical meaning in the society where Alun Cilie and his neighbours Wil and Elin lived. 'They lived on *cardod*,' writes David Jenkins (ibid p. 62), 'referring to the buttermilk, swedes, and oatmeal cottagers received at farms and which were a part of their returns for the work debt that they paid.' Cottagers in this context means people who had no land themselves, and in Alun Cilie's *Enemies*, we enter the world of a couple, Wil and Elin, who are seeking to join a higher social class by cultivating a piece of untamed land.

David Jenkins describes the poverty such a couple would have endured in Ceredigion in the early 20th century. (Here the term 'horse-place' is a synonym for a small farm): 'The years during which a young couple held a horse-place were their most difficult for they had to collect sufficient capital to establish themselves on a farm if they were ever to join the ranks of 'farmers'. It was necessary to make clothes last whatever their condition, to retire for the night before it was necessary to use a light, to ride the workhorse with nothing on the animal's back but a sack in order to save the expense of a saddle, and in some cases to scrape the encrustation of salt from the salted bacon in order to re-use it' (Jenkins, p. 87).

Whereas clearing the land is one theme in the work of the Ceredigion poets, and the joy of seeing a once barren hillside or overgrown valley produce crops, the mountain and the woods will soon reclaim the green acre if allowed. In

Golygfa o'r Gaer Ddu (*A View from Caer Ddu*), written in 1915, Isfoel describes a tract of land returning to a state of wilderness. He sees the estate in the distance, and the raised bank of land nearby, and is saddened by the decline. Along the paths where hay once grew, wild animals raise their cubs. The fox is rampant, the badger too, rabbits burrow into the slopes, briar and fern cast their net, and extensive growth bars the way.

The boundary between wilderness and farmland is rich in tension and in symbolism, and in a poem entitled *Clawdd* (*Wall*) Alun Cilie writes how a man comes to mark the boundary of a field. With deft hand he strings the stones together to build his wall, and crowns it with a thorn bush to break the east-wind. Within this boundary, the world is ordered and functional, and man the farmer can fulfil his potential and feel that his life is a dignified one. This gives rise to feelings described, again by Alun Cilie, in the poem *Yr Amaethwr* (*The Farmer*) whose daily joy is to ready his horse, to follow his plough where the green shoot emerges in the warmth of the sun's rays, and to see the hedges wear their green gown. He sees his fields wide as the emerald sea, and awaits the heave and sway of the harvest where the glinting blade passes in spring. His to enjoy is the lavish praise of the soil where once he toiled and strained.

In *Yr Arloeswr* (*The Pioneer*), Dafydd Jones Ffair Rhos writes a passage called *Cân y Ffin* (*Song of the Boundary*). The boundary wall, writes Dafydd Jones, is a solid wall to keep the wild animals at bay. It provides shelter for the feeble lambs when hail sweeps the mountain in spring. Cattle shelter there when the summer is at its height, and an occasional couple come there to court. A blade-thin lattice-work, the wall divides the open spaces of the plains into handsome estates.

In *Y Comin* (*The Common*), Dafydd Jones describes the

uncultivated land beyond fence and boundary. An unowned place, he calls it, where weeds prosper and the toothed harrow does not tear the sod, so that the shoot may grow in the sunlight. The gypsies go there in summer, and smoke rises lazily from their fires in the midst of the rushes. The common, he writes, is an unsightly place where the lone kestrel hunts. It is a no-man's land, a wilderness of worthless acres where Abraham Wood lives, a synonym in Welsh for the landless itinerant.

In *Yr Hen Fyd* (*The Old World*), the final poem of his book *The Pioneer,* Dafydd Jones writes poignantly of good land being lost to the wilderness as time passes, and of things he knew that are disappearing. On the mountains in Ffair Rhos, he sees the twisted briars growing on the ridges and casting their net over paths of old. They do not fear the swinging scythe, seeking only to ruin the farmer's work.

Isgarn and Dafydd Jones, the former in South Ceredigion by the coast, the latter in the mountains further north, both witness cultivated land reclaimed by nature, and their reaction is tinged with melancholy. However, David Jenkins (p. 17) tells us that '...in purely agricultural parishes in south-west Wales the population declined consistently from 1841 until the Second World War', and that 'even with a slight recovery by 1951, the population was then little more than it was in 1801 when the first census was taken'. Given these facts, some loss of land once cleared was no doubt inevitable. In *The Pioneer,* Dafydd Jones records this chapter in history in lines that ring loud. On these hills, he writes, the miracle of the smallholding is nearing its end, and the ruined houses are returning to the warm bosom of the peaty earth.

On the other side of the mountains, near the market-town of Tregaron, John Roderick Rees, also visits the theme of an abandoned smallholding. The poem is called *Y*

Murddun (*The Ruin*). He describes a cottage and garden disintegrating there in peace. This, he states, is the fate of a century of smallholdings.

One of the best known poems on this theme is *Rhos Helyg* by Ben T. Hopkins. Hopkins was born in 1897 in Lledrod, central Ceredigion, and is associated with nearby Mynydd Bach, an upland area of open commonage and windswept farmland. A selection of his work is extant in a slim volume forty-six pages long entitled *Rhos Helyg a Cherddi Eraill* (*Rhos Helyg and Other Poems*). The thrust of the title poem *Rhos Helyg* (*Willow Hill*) is direct. Where once there was a garden, B.T. Hopkins sees land where the briars grow in abundance, and where the soil is rough and unploughed. Rushes grow there, and it yields no grain. Verse three tells how in Rhos Helyg the hearth where a fire once burned bright has now grown cold. The fresh open ground has vanished, replaced by grey tracts of land. The meadow in Rhos Helyg is pale, forlorn and still, and the sweet odour of hay is no more.

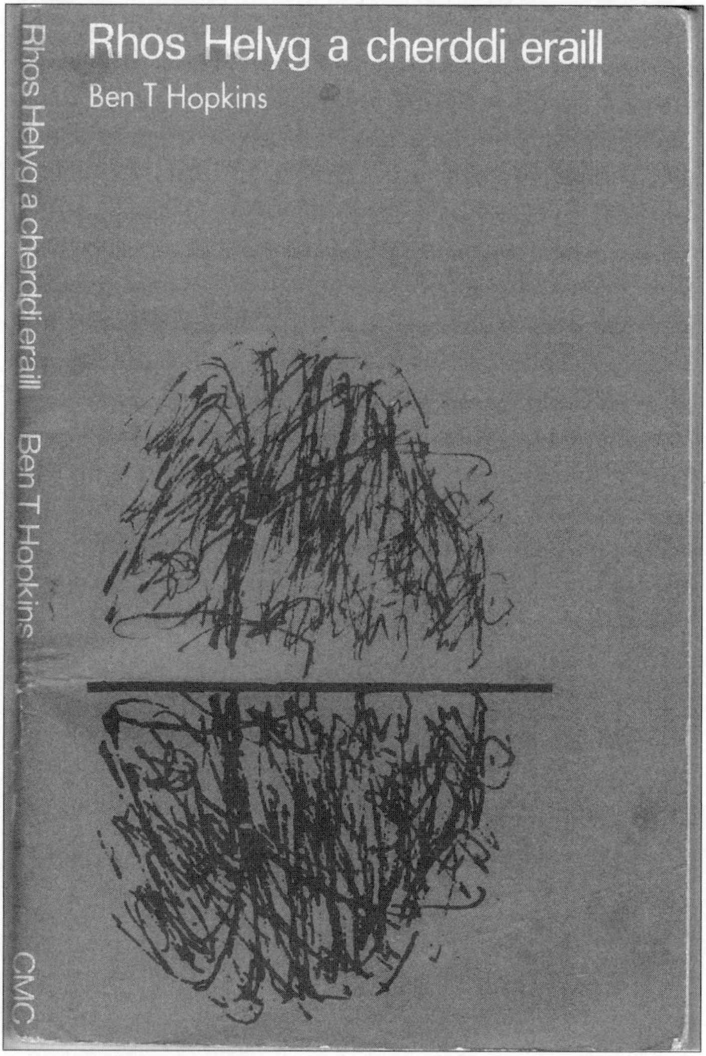
Rhos Helyg a cherddi eraill
Ben T Hopkins
Rhos Helyg a cherddi eraill
Ben T Hopkins
CMC

Land Gained, Land Relinquished – Four Phases of Ownership

The work of the rural bards of Ceredigion in the 20th century reveals four phases in the history of the land, its productivity and ownership of it. In the first phase, during the mid-nineteenth century, the land is owned by the aristocracy, and the poor tenant builds his *tŷ unnos* on mountain commonage. Here, a man could claim a certain territory on condition that he build a house in one night, and that smoke rise from the chimney by sun-rise. Such *tai unnos* were built in Ceredigion. The opening lines of Dafydd Jones' *Yr Arloeswr* ('*The Pioneer*') relate how, bitten by the dawn frost, one such man came to claim a holding, to mark out its green boundaries, and ultimately to pave the by-road that led there.

The society that grew up around the *tai unnos* proved to be economically unstable. The *tyddynwyr* – crofters – came to accept that to survive they must supplement their income. From Mynydd Bach and Tregaron, the people, especially the men, migrated to the South, sometimes on a seasonal basis, to work in the coal-mines, for example. Some stayed at home, despite the poverty and the limited prospects. These include Siâms in the poem *Calan Mai* (*May Day*), a man, writes John Roderick Rees, who knows nothing of the abandon with which May is celebrated in the mining valleys, or of the sour taste of coal-dust in the air that sets the teeth on edge. Siâms and his ilk do know other things however. After long winter months, they can tell to the hour when the cow will cease to stare hungrily from the byre, and sense the earth awakening.

Of the women who stayed in the region, some worked as maids in various local manor houses. In the poem *Unigedd* (*Solitude*) by John Roderick Rees, we read of one such, a girl who leaves home aged twelve, and returns forty years later to an empty house. From dawn to dusk, year in year out, writes the poet, Sara washed flagstone floors and all the children's clothes, boiling vatfuls of water and baking bread for her masters.

In Ffair Rhos, the native village of W.J. Gruffydd, mines were opened in the nineteenth century. These provided employment for local people, as did mines in the uplands of north Ceredigion from Ffair Rhos northward to Gogerddan, Cwmsymlog and Tal-y-bont. This mining activity polluted the waters of north Ceredigion, and several of its rivers from Ystwyth to the Dyfi, an inheritance being corrected only today by modern cleaning technology. In *Unigedd* (*Solitude*), W.J. Gruffydd refers to this industrial side-effect. He speaks of strontium in the drizzle in Pant y Blaidd, and poisonous dust bringing death to the pastures. It is a poison that finds its way to the marrow of the sheep's bone and even into the milk of the cow.

Writing of Ffair Rhos and the Ceredigion uplands in the early decades of the 20th century, W.J. Gruffydd practices a distinctive brand of rural realism. In *Ffenestri* (*Windows*), we visit with him a shimmering moor in the mountains where, plagued by maggots, a sheep approaches a pool in the bog to squirm and writhe in the summer heat, before a shower of rain finally disperses an army of flies and turns the dry earth to slime. He portrays an old cart-house, wearied by many winters, its rafters little more than a battered ribcage, falling as it were to one knee to await the onslaught of the final gale.

This brand of Welsh-language rural realism is practiced not only by W.J. Gruffydd, but also by John Roderick Rees. Gruffydd and Roderick Rees were born in 1920 and 1916 respectively, and died in 2009 and 2011. Both men were from the mid-Ceredigion uplands near Tregaron. Each won more than one coveted prize at the national *eisteddfod*. Both men wrote of the small farmers – *tyddynnwyr* – of their native area, and of their struggle to eke a living out of a hostile environment. Both were also educated, W.J. Gruffydd as a preacher, John Roderick Rees a teacher. Both men lost both mother and father while they were still very young.

Certain differences in their careers are apparent. W.J. Gruffydd was well-known nationally in his day as an *eisteddfod*-goer and Arch-druid. John Roderick Rees was less involved in public life. W.J. Gruffydd's career as a poet spans a relatively short mid-life period. John Roderick Rees continued to compose long after his retirement. W. J. Gruffydd, in his later years, enjoyed the success of a series of light prose books where he describes with much wit and humour the lives of an elderly couple, Tomos and Marged, who live in a remote village near Ffair Rhos. Gruffydd also wrote an autobiography in his twilight years. John Roderick Rees wrote no prose, apart from diaries and letters, none of which have yet been published. The work of these two men, neighbours, rivals at times, but brothers in letters, records the cycle of ownership of the land in Ceredigion.

The second phase begins during William Gladstone's second term as Prime Minister in the 1880s, when patterns of land-ownership are challenged. In the ensuing decades more land begins to fall to the small farmer and to the common people. Over the next three generations, the people proudly work the land, bringing it to fruition, latterly with the help of modern machines. The word *tyddyn* – the croft, the smallholding – is central to the world of the rural poet in 20th century West Wales. During the second phase of ownership, the *tyddynwr* or small-holder has established himself, drained his few acres, and planted his crops. In *Y Winllan*, for example, a long poem that documents the social and agricultural history in Bethania, Tregaron, John

Roderick Rees writes of the conquest of the land after the building of the *tŷ unnos*. With his trusted spade, weary at end of day, the former tenant carves out the boundary of his own modest holding, hoping that grey oats will soon grow in the peaty earth.

Gelynion (Enemies), a long poem by Alun Cilie, describes the struggle of Wil yr Hafod, a smallholder – *tyddynwr* – to bring barren land to fruition. In one verse we read of Wil's labours as he clears the stubborn, old hedgerow bushes, taming his land with raw strength and determination, until its acres are readied for the seed.

In the third phase of the cycle, the earth yields the fullness of its harvest. This fulfilment is a recurring theme in the corpus. In *Cynhaeaf* (*Harvest*), Dic Jones writes of the harvest in his own day, the third quarter of the 20th century, an era of further mechanisation of the farmers' work. He describes the trees at Michaelmas, yellow in a grey mist that hangs over the neck of the valley. The thresher, slow and train-like, has vented its Homeric roar, fading now into the deepened twilight, as it does this and every autumn, leaving on the lane for all to see a track of chaff to mark the passage of its wheels.

In Dic Jones' *Harvest,* a poem firmly rooted in rural Wales, we find lines universal in their appeal, and images that transcend the local environment. In his celebrated ode, or *awdl* in Welsh, the poet remarks that husbandry will continue to be practiced as long as man walks the earth, and that the next generation, heir of past generations, will assume its succession. While winter still comes and goes, while the harvest is gathered in, and while the soil is worked, there will be sustenance for living things. The world, he says, will know fertility as long as the sun shines and the dew continues to fall.

Yr un yw Calon Hael y Ddaear Hen (*The Earth has a*

selfless and unchanging Heart), an unfinished twelve-line sonnet by Alun Cilie, is similar in tenor to passages from Dic Jones' *Harvest*. The earth, writes Alun Cilie, shall always smile anew where scarred by the scythe. Its bounty remains although its children pursue their many paths. And come what may, she shall bestow on us the goodness of her many treasures.

The fourth phase in the history of land-ownership in Ceredigion, as documented in the work of the rural poets, is the relinquishing and abandonment of certain small holdings, houses and land by the people, and the purchase of some of these by incoming English settlers. The cycle is complete: land won in the late 19th century is land forfeit three generations later. In *Llygaid* (*Eyes*), John Roderick Rees writes of a holding called Pen-Cnwc. Long the haunt of owls, moss has been slowly colonising it for many years since it was abandoned. But the dampness fails to take hold and stain the walls with its funerary wreath, and despite forty years of rain the slates have held fast. Through wind and foul weather, the house has resisted decay, solidly built as it was by Welsh hands that have now passed on.

First its beginnings, next the coming of age, now follows the demise of the community, the abandonment of the old houses, and the age of the English incomer. The poem *Calan Gaeaf* (*Winter's Eve*) captures a moment in time when things lie in the balance. John Roderick Rees introduces us to Siâms yr Hafod, asking us to show him some compassion. His sheaves may be coarse and brittle, but the task is daunting and the land unforgiving. Forty acres of clay, writes the poet, weigh heavy on his and his wife's hands. Another paltry harvest-season is ending, but there is no promise of recompense for the year's work, nothing to rattle in the purse. The outhouses and land tell the story of changing fortunes, and the stable-door is dotted with names carved while waiting for a shower to pass. Though never prosperous, Siâms yr Hafod remains undeterred, writes John Roderick Rees. Without help however, he cannot survive much longer, and Twm, the last farmhand in Yr Hafod, has already moved to town to work there, emptying ash from the bins.

Some of the *tyddynwyr* left, others stayed to be buried in the soil to which they had devoted their lives, but ultimately the society seemed bound to stagnate. The homesteads become a place in the past. W.J. Gruffydd begins *Ffenestri* (*Windows*) with the motif of return to the deserted homestead. From Bwlch-y-Gwynt to Ffair Rhos Square he climbs the protracted mile over the steep hump to lands where rush and heather stand guard over the old ruins of Pen-Cwm-Bach. The way is just long enough to sing a popular tune called Tôn-y-Botel. When the houses appear in the secluded valley, their windows are sockets in the walls with neither glass nor pane, like the sockets in a skull staring across the peat lands. When the moon rises, sly and ghostly, above Esgair Garn, one could mistake the shadows for movement in one of the houses, somebody carrying a prying candle from kitchen to parlour perhaps, and delaying by the window until a cloud darkens the moon. But life within the confines of this place belong to a time firmly in the past when, one wet afternoon, the last tenant left, pace unhurried, in a horse-drawn funeral carriage round the turn in Lôn Groes road.

ISGARN

Caniadau Isgarn

DETHOLIAD GYDA RHAGYMADRODD

GAN

YR ATHRO T. H. PARRY-WILLIAMS

A GWERTHFAWROGIAD

GAN

S. M. POWELL

ABERYSTWYTH

1949

The Mechanisation of Agriculture

In a short autobiography that prefaces Isfoel's second volume of verse, the author dedicates two pages to the description of machines introduced into the area during the period 1891 to 1920. He remembers his father buying a machine to make hay together with a neighbour in 1891. 'An old Cambrian Mower – a big, noisy machine,' he writes, and 'a terrible burden for horses', He then describes the local farmers gathering to cast a critical eye on the contraption. Despite early resistance to innovation however, 'the countryside,' he writes, 'underwent a period of Genesis.' The arrival of new devices and machines was 'like a hurricane' that 'swept venerated old tools aside' for ever.

One of the new appliances that helped to revolutionise farming around the turn of the century was the mechanised thrashing machine. The machine was transported from farm to farm, and the thrashing, Isfoel writes, 'was done on the yard', saving the labourers from the stale and unhealthy atmosphere of dark, unventilated barns'. The advent of these machines heralded the demise of the horse. Isfoel provides the following anecdote: one farmer asks another how many horses he has on the farm. 'Not a single one,' comes the reply, 'we ate them all months ago.'

Of all the many modern machines that contributed to the industrialisation of agriculture in the early and mid-20th century, the tractor was undoubtedly the most influential. 'We got a tractor in 1920,' writes Isfoel, 'and it was of great comfort to us to work the land, and to tow our machines'. It also relieved the horses of some of the heavier labour to which they had traditionally been subject. Isfoel notes, and expresses his surprise that no other farmer in the locality opted to acquire a tractor for a good ten years after the first model appeared in Cilie Farm in South Ceredigion in 1920.

David Jenkins (p. 262) comments on the staggered arrival of the tractor on farms in Ceredigion: 'The first tractors came in 1917, in connection with the Agricultural Committees established during the First World War, and the first privately owned tractors soon after the end of the war. The depression of the 1920s and 1930s slowed down the rate at which at which tractors were purchased, and it was not until the years following the Second World War that they completely replaced horses for farm-work'.

We find evidence for the replacement of horse by tractor in the work of several of the rural poets of Ceredigion. A well-known poem in its day on the theme of obsolete farm implements by Alun Cilie is called *Sgrap* (*Scrap*). One afternoon, the poet gathers the relics of yesteryear from all over the farm, bits of old gear that no longer have their place in the modern age. From stable and carthouse he extracts box-carts, a jaunt, a trap, horse-drawn ploughs, single-furrow and double, all of which are thrown together in disarray on the scrapheap.

The sonnet *Sgrap* brings to mind *Chwalu* (*Destruction*) by a brother of Alun Cilie's, the mariner S.B. Jones. The poem is a 'double-sonnet' written in 1936, when the old house at Cilie Farm was replaced by a modern building. Hand in hand with the modernisation of agriculture went the replacement of many older houses by new buildings. The poem affords a good description of certain features of the doomed old house. The walls are knocked down with sledge-hammer and with bolt, the oak beams and the roof stripped bare. The clay fireplaces are ripped out, together with the great chimney hood, caked thick with soot.

Old things rotting in barn and stable are described too by John Roderick Rees. In a poem called *Pony and Trap*, for example, the jaunt lies covered by the spider's web, its lattice framework a mesh of tiny holes made by the gnawing of the woodlice and turning its brittle skeleton into firewood.

John Roderick Rees, like with his father and grandfather before him, was involved in breeding and rearing Welsh Cobs, a handsome race of plough-horse synonymous with the county. In the poem *Nhad* (*My Father*), he writes of his father's love and undivided passion for the breed, naming him the prince of their tradition, a man fully versed in the complexities of their lineage, and master of equine lore. John Roderick Rees writes of his grandfather that he dedicated his life to the romance of the Welsh Cob, immersing himself in what the poet colourfully calls 'the *mabinogi* of the horse', a reference to medieval myth and romance.

The pride of a family tradition is distilled in the poem *Brenin Gwalia* (*King of Gwalia*), a eulogy to a famous stallion of that name. *Brenin Gwalia* was brought to London to an international show and applauded rapturously by no fewer than a crowd of eighty thousand people, we are told in the poem. During my visits to the poet's house in the years before his death, John Roderick Rees spoke again of Brenin Gwalia at the London show, the king of a race bred in the distant hills. An anecdote in the oral tradition tells how, while learning to drive a car with a fellow Ceredigion man, the poet, rather than applying the brakes, cried 'Wo!' to encourage the car to stop.

David Jenkins (p. 104) writes of local respect for the men who knew about horses: '...it was high praise for any farmer to be known as a 'man of horses' (*dyn ceffyle*), which did not so much mean 'horseman' as a man who was known for his personal capacity to assess horses and to care for them'.

Remaining with the theme of horse and tractor, we find *Atgofion* (*Memories*), a poem in which J.R. Jones writes of two horses, 'Star' and 'Brown'. The poet remembers Brown and Star bowing low on the heath, his father holding the reins fast, the horses' massive fetlocks making the clay roll, the strength of their three years showing in the sheen of their coats. This image from a time past returned to him unexpectedly one May at noon as he drove his tractor through Cae Gwynt gap. He remembers too the day his father sold the horses, commenting that, when he shook hands on the bargain, more than just a pair of old mares were sent away.

Alun Cilie writes on the same theme in *Fy Ngwedd Geffylau Olaf,* (*My Last Pair of Draught Horses*). He expresses his dispassion regarding the wonderful but lonely tractor. Put out to grass on the rougher land of Pant-y-Ci far from ridge and furrow, the horses seem to sense what has happened, and they turn their buttocks to the wind when they chance to see the poet pass.

Lines from *Cywydd y Tractor* (*The Song of the Tractor*) by Isfoel tells how the tractor conquers the idle, age-old moorland, climbing with plough and harrow to the upland marsh where the hare roams. The tractor increases productivity, and from the wasteland a crop of oats appears where the blade gashed the earth.

In the book *Yr Arloeswr* (*The Pioneer*), Dafydd Jones Ffair Rhos also marks the transition from horse to tractor in a poem entitled *Yr Amaethwr* (*The Farmer*). Where once he braved the icy wind with a pair of good draught horses, he no longer comes now to ply the yoke. The tractor has replaced the horse in Ffair Rhos too, and now, along the winding lane through a gap in the bank, the farmer drives into the clearing, and with his machine opens fallow land to receive the seed.

Two poems in our corpus, *Gwynfyd* (Utopia) by Alun Cilie, and *Arddwr* (*Ploughing a Furrow*) by John Roderick Rees record the equivalent of an initiation rite that was central to the culture of horse and plough. In both texts, boy becomes man as he drives the plough for the first time. Writing of the clear division of labour between men and women in the agricultural community in South-West Wales at the turn of the 20th century, David Jenkins makes the following remarks (p. 76): 'The prestige work which was described as 'the highest work of the farm' (*gwaith ucha'r ffarm*) belonged to the men. Their work fell into two major parts, the work of cultivation which entailed working with horses (which was the 'highest work') and the general labouring necessary to maintain and improve the farm's physical condition'. Significantly however, Jenkins draws attention to the fact that, within the male-dominated world of horse and plough, not the older men but rather the younger sit atop the hierarchy: 'Yet the 'highest work' of the farm was the work of usually young and unmarried men, the farm servants. A farmer could not take one of his own horses without the permission of the head servant who was responsible for the horses. If he did, it was regarded as sufficient reason for the servant to break his contract of employment'.

In *Gwynfyd* (*Utopia*), Alun Cilie captures the thrill of his own initiation into the adult world. One splendid spring morning, when the poet was a youthful fourteen years old, the best pair of horses in the stable between his hands, he ventured into the field alone for the first time. His utopia was to hear the earth turning and tearing under his feet as its fresh scent filled his lungs, and the thrill quickening his blood.

Arddwr (*Ploughing a Furrow*) by John Roderick Rees deals with the same theme. The poet imagines the scene, addressing first the horses, then the boy. He calls on the horses to make no haste, reminding them that a boy is driving the plough, and calling to mind that the harp-shaped field they are ploughing. Cae Delyn, he says, while somewhat shallow, is living soil every inch. The youth is reminded of the tradition he now upholds. He walks the furrow his fathers made between the shafts of his sleek plough. For more than a century, the poet tells him, his people's vitality has been resonating here in this strip of soil.

In Alun Cilie's posthumous *Cerddi Pentalar,* the poem *Hiraeth* (*Yearning*), the poet longs for times of old before the roar of the motor. Perched on his belching tractor, what can the modern farmer know, he asks, of the quiet thrill that quickens the heart when a man proudly grasps the shafts of his plough?

In the work of J.M. Edwards, the texts *Molawd y Pridd* (*In Praise of the Soil*) and *Y Preimin* (*The Premium*) transport us into the pre-industrial world of plough and furrow. In the first, a section called *Cân yr Aradrwr* (*Ploughman's Song*) reveals lines such as the following, addressed, not to a lover or a deity, but to the very soil. 'In the stoneless temple of the wind, and in the rolling rainfields, I sing your praises, echo your renown, and state for you my passion.'

Nowhere in the corpus is the timeless union between man and soil more evident than here. The use of literary forms and of erudite vocabulary, reminiscent of Biblical prose, all woven into the monologue of a simple ploughman, lend certain passages in the poem an air distinctly psalm-like. A simple English equivalent of one such passage might read as follows: 'The sustenance that you possess deep within your bosom is the place that harbours all our dreams, and from your mysterious dark, the joy of harvest-song will emerge the world over.'

The second text by J.M. Edwards, *Y Preimin,* is less mystical, and describes in detail an annual ploughing contest held in February. The poem takes its name from a prize, the 'premium', originally offered by Thomas Johnes (1748–1816) of Hafod Uchtryd, Ceredigion, for good crops produced by local farmers. The word 'premium' passed into the Welsh language locally, and remained current for two centuries until horse and plough made way for the machine.

J.M. Edwards writes that of all the days of the calendar, there was none that thrilled them more than the ploughing contest. The young men congregated enthusiastically to take part in the event. Carts of every colour stand in rows at the head of Dolau Mawr field. The poet lists the names of the farms represented; Blaen Esgair, Wern Fach, Llain, Morfa Mawr, Glyngynwydd, Maes Llyn, Rhyd Hir, Dôl Gain, Y Llethrau, Rhos Llwyd and Bryn Gwyn. Each name paints a picture. The sound of harness and chain rings in the keen wind. This is a community, writes J.M. Edwards, bound together by the perennial sounds of its rural arms. The poem, some five hundred words long, ends at the close of day as a timid February moon appears to smile upon the virgin soil. For centuries the moon has visited this scene, yet its mystery remains intact, so old and yet so fresh.

A second poem on this theme is *Yr Ymryson Aredig* (*The Ploughing Contest*) by John Roderick Rees. Whereas nostalgia tinged with a certain gravitas characterises some of the retrospective work of the period, this text is overtly ironic, and, written in the popular *triban* metre, the rhyme in the Welsh original seems to smile at the reader. The poet remembers the plough a certain Deio had whose shafts were slippery as soap. Despite this, the work done was quite commendable, the ploughed strips are straight and true, and the tidy head-furrows open out into in a neat pattern.

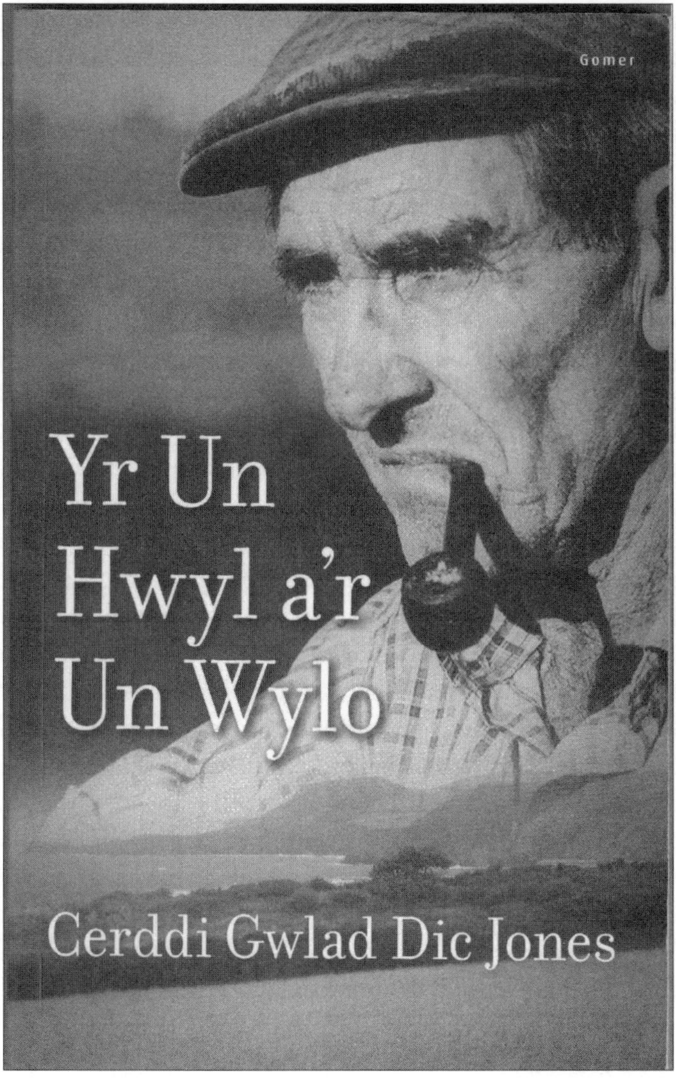
Gomer
Yr Un
Hwyl a'r
Un Wylo
Cerddi Gwlad Dic Jones

The Harvesters

The mechanisation of agricultural work increased productivity, eliminated labour, and reduced the time and manpower necessary to complete many tasks. However, despite its many blessings, it brought the isolation of the farmer from his fellows, and the end of customs and practices that provided social cohesion and human interaction. In the pre-mechanised world, the people pooled their resources to overcome an often hostile environment, rejoicing when their efforts bore fruit. In the post-manual world, each man is sovereign on his farm, but tends as he works to be alienated from the rest of society.

David Jenkins (pp 3-4) writes of pre-mechanical harvest scenes he witnessed in Ceredigion in the mid-twentieth century: 'In 1953, I counted thirty-five people engaged in the hay harvest of an 8-acre holding. They worked from mid-day till seven o'clock in the evening with none of the equipment that has long been common on larger holdings'. He also recounts the following experience: 'During the summer of 1959 I watched men cutting corn with a scythe and binding it by hand in a North Cardiganshire valley within twelve miles of Aberystywth. As late as 1951, the reaping hook was used in mid Cardiganshire to save the crop during a difficult harvest'.

The Welsh word for this group of harvest-workers is *medel.* The word is ancient, and cognate with *meitheal,* an equivalent used in Irish for a group of workers. By now, it has now disappeared from spoken Welsh, and speakers born after 1950 are in general not acquainted with it. The *medel* however is central to the society in which our bards and poets grew up.

In *Y Cynhaeaf* (*The Harvest*), Alun Cilie describes scenes such as those witnessed by David Jenkins. The poet, born in 1898, is still a boy in the poem, and the time in question typifies harvest-time in Southern Ceredigion between 1900 and the First World War. The poet remembers wondering why the cobbler's fingers seemed so gnarled and blackened early in the day, not realising that, late into the night, he sat at his bench, turning the thick thread and working the wax. The boy-poet wondered too at the old weaver, his waistcoat a crust of bright stalks, as he set the blade and handle of his scythe. The weaver's eyes gleamed, and he worked eagerly, having taken leave of his racing loom for one momentous harvest-day.

David Jenkins (p. 91) writes of the importance of the harvest as a social occasion: 'They were days when more conversational liberties than usual were allowed, and while sitting at ease after tea, which was taken in the hayfield, a man might tussle with a maid in full view of the others present, throw her on the hay, and kiss her'. This practice, he says, was known as 'foxing' (*ffocso*)'.

In *Y Cynhaeaf* (*The Harvest*) by Alun Cilie, a poem some 130 lines in length, we find a lively description of the atmosphere in the field. He hears a shout of joy as the food-basket arrives. The woman bringing the meal wears an apron bright as a stoat's breast as she appears in a gap in the hedge. The billowing linen-cloth is shaken open, and the provisions spread out on the very ground. Then it is time to sit and rest, and praise the hand that had prepared the feast. As the poem continues, we are introduced to both the men and women who return the following day, buoyant and in high spirits. And there are the shy exchanges between maid and farm-hand that melt into the whispering of the brittle stooks.

Almost half a century later, in scenes described by Dic Jones in *Cynhaeaf* (*Harvest*), the machine has been integrated into a way of life, and the thresher vents its roar over the fields leaving a track of chaff on the lane to mark its passage. Writing in the late 1960s, the poet and farmer pauses now to pay tribute to a by-gone age, remembering his fathers who once strode the hollows, pursuing their task and bound together by their labour. In their day, they replenished the soil, filling their carts with fertile goodness, and thanks not only to mechanisation and progress, but also to their labour and efforts, the fruit of the earth now flows forth.

As a child in the years before The Second World War, Dic Jones too witnessed the collective spirit the of pre-mechanised agricultural world. He describes these memories in a further passage from *Harvest*, recalling once more the neighbourly company, the unhurried reaping-party, their ready hands practicing the age-old craft of making stooks and binding sheaves. All spoke Welsh, and the old language paraded full of mirth in its working clothes. But by the late 1960s, times had changed. The poet reflects on the mechanisation of agricultural and the changes it has ushered in, commenting that from the modern tractor-seat, husbandry has become a more leisurely pursuit. And whereas once the whole community made their way to the golden fields in August to stack the handsome crop, today the work can be done by a mere two men.

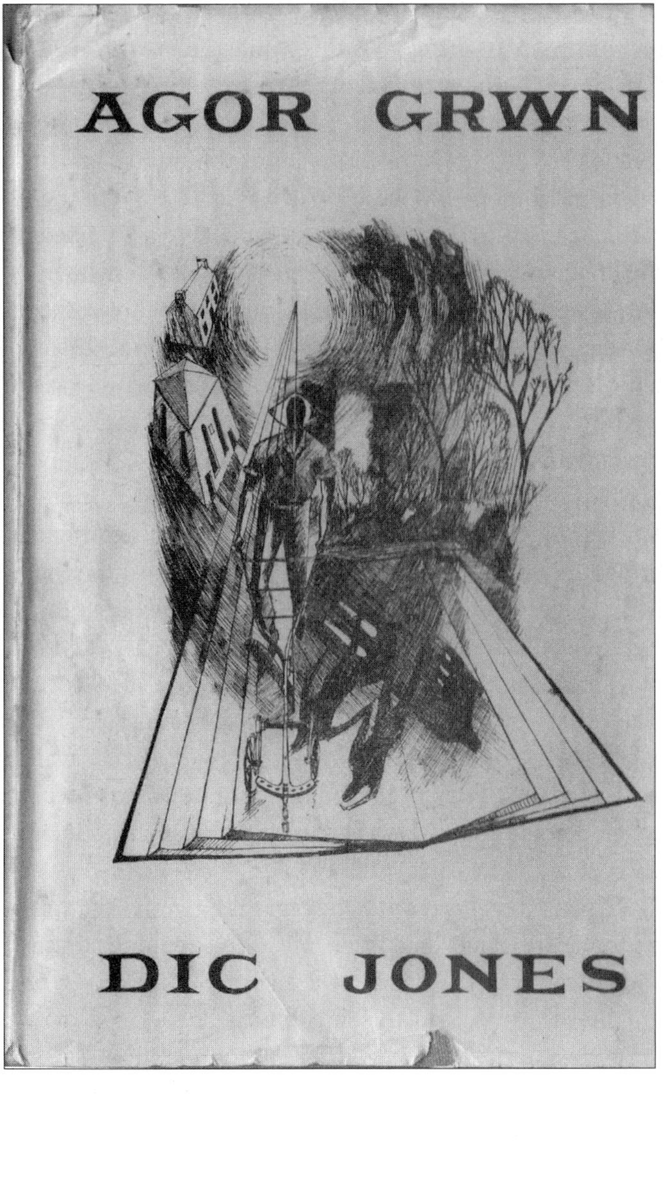
AGOR GRWN
DIC JONES

The Mechanisation of Dairying

For the first fifty years or so of our period, from about 1880 to 1930, dairying in Ceredigion was part of the responsibility of the womenfolk, while the men worked with the horses. With the arrival of the tractor, this order of things was brought into question, and change soon set in. David Jenkins (p. 262) tells us more about the tradition: '...it was the farm women who were closely associated with the milk cattle, while the men of the household were associated with the horses. Men would accept employment as cowmen only if they were unable to find posts as servants, who worked the horses. It was considered an insult for a man to have to milk. Unless the women cleaned the cow stalls the work was done by the second servant or 'lad', the 'petty servant' who was the lowest in the hierarchy of male farm workers.

Jenkins (p. 262) explains how the Agricultural Marketing Acts of 1931 and 1933 were instrumental in bringing change about: 'It was with the establishment of the Milk Marketing Board, under the provisions of the Agricultural Marketing Acts of 1931 and 1933, that the sale of milk in bulk became common-place.' He also notes (p. 261) that 'by the time the Milk Marketing Board was established, young women were no longer readily available as farm maids. They preferred to emigrate, or to enter what other employment was available'. And so, he concludes, 'dairy work came to an end'.

These developments meant that, while the tractor replaced the horse, dairying evolved to become an industry, and passed into the hands of the men. Soon the size of the milk-herd grows, and the milk-churns are placed daily on the milk-stand, *stand la'th* in Welsh, at the junction of the lane leading to the farm-house and the public road to be collected by the lorry.

Traditions associated with dairying were bound to become obsolete. David Jenkins (p. 104) describes an example: 'It appears that according to an old practice which had almost disappeared by the late nineteenth century that it was the eldest daughter who named the calves'. 'Cattle invariably had Welsh names', he writes, 'while most horses bore English names'. This is born out in our texts: the horses J.R. Jones writes of, for example, are called 'Star' and 'Brown'.

Of the very few texts in the corpus that discuss dairying or the milk industry in any way, one is *Y Bwrdd* (*The Board*) by John Roderick Rees, a reference to The Milk Marketing Board. Whereas the poems that deal with ploughing and horses are rich in technical vocabulary, and intimate in their nature, this text is plain and dispassionate, reading rather like a series of jottings or notes, but with rhyme. In the nineteen thirties, he writes, in the mountain dwellings and in the old homesteads, scraping together the rent and the wages was a difficult task. Some pioneers foresaw a cooperative structure as the path to salvation. Soon lorries could be heard sounding their horns in the valleys, and new-found riches rang in the milk-cans.

In another poem by Alun Cilie, *Gwerthu Llaeth* (*Selling Milk*), a new milking parlour replaces the old. The poet admits that this represents an improvement. The cattle are no longer tied by ropes, their hooves are not covered in muck and slime, nor are their sides and rumps caked in excrement. The poet remembers too how the dung-beetles would suck the blood under the hide of the cattle in the old parlour. However, radical change and progress bring with them a trauma of their own. The poem culminates with the following couplet. 'The empty benches in the cool of the back dairy, and the wooden butter-dish look at me accusingly, calling me a fool.' The wooden butter-dish,

Welsh *noe,* was a relic of a former time, and was an implement used by the women in their dairying work. This poem by Alun Cilie is one of many where we see time balanced finely between yesteryear and a mechanised future.

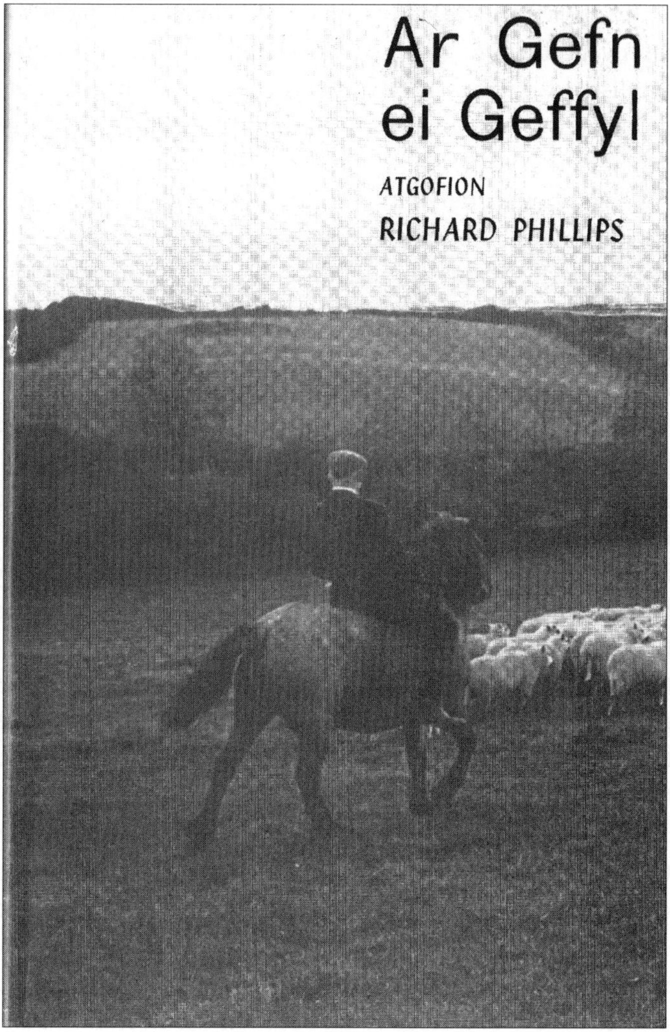
Ar Gefn
ei Geffyl
ATGOFION
RICHARD PHILLIPS

Welsh Faces of Their Time

Who are the people we meet in the work of the 20th century Ceredigion poets? Whose are the names and faces we discover? Beyond the generic craftsman, the archetypal small-holder, the good ploughman and the diligent blacksmith, how much warmth, how much fear and hope can be detected in this extensive corpus? Balanced between the beauty and order of its classical metre and idiom, and the fresh, convivial humour of its bardic community, the Welsh verse inherited from Ceredigion in the 20th century seldom removes the mask of convention, seldom portrays the naked flame of individual lives, seldom shines a bright light on the reality of the human condition.

Taken together however, the poems that do follow this path form an important sub-group where the characters of rural Wales in the early 20th century come briefly and vividly to life. This sub-group includes the following texts: *Ffynnonsewyl* by Isfoel (*Ail Gerddi,* p. 41); *Nani Ffebi* by Isfoel (*Ail Gerddi,* p. 65); *Gelynion* (*Enemies*) by Alun Cilie (*Cerddi,* p. 14); *Glannau* (*Banks*) by John Roderick Rees (*Cerddi Newydd,* p. 20); *Unigedd* (*Solitude*) by John Roderick Rees (*Cerddi,* p. 118); *Unigedd* (*Solitude*) by W.J. Gruffydd, (*Ffenestri,* p 67); *Y Pasg* (*Easter*) by J.R. Jones (*Cerddi* J.R. p. 53).

Ffynnonsewyl is a place in the Cothi Valley, in North Carmarthenshire where Isfoel in his younger days would visit members of his wider family. The poem, simple and undramatic, transports us into a Welsh household in the late nineteenth century. Isfoel tells of Rhys and Nan, who lived near the brow of a steep road, between the river Cothi and Llanfynydd village, in a cottage called Ffynnonsewyl, Sewyl's Well. The poem gives insight into the life of farm-hands and housemaids who would call by on their way home, dressed still in their working clothes, and entering, according to Welsh custom, without knocking or even calling 'hello'. Life in the Cothi Valley was markedly communal, and at night when the clock had been rewound and the wristwatch placed on the dresser, the two, Rhys and Nan, would drag themselves off to bed in full view of the company who remained until the last embers of the fire had died.

In the poem *Nani Ffebi,* we are given a glimpse of an elderly woman who spends time visiting other houses like that of Rhys and Nan of Ffynnonsewyl. The poem includes a very late allusion to the custom of women in Wales knitting while walking. Reference to Blaencelyn would seem to date the poem to 1889 or earlier, during the years before Jeremiah Jones moved the family to Cilie Farm. Isfoel (*Ail Gerddi,* p. 65) remembers seeing Nani Ffebi, a lively old girl, crossing over the ridge at Blaencelyn to take afternoon tea and enjoy a chat with one of the neighbours. The sock she carried with her was unfinished and the knitting needles clicked busily.

Gelynion by Alun Cilie is a more earnest affair. The poem is 39 quatrains long. It tells in verse the story of Wil yr Hafod and his wife Elin who pit their strength against the elements, against fate and against all odds to make of poor bog land a good small-holding. In verse 7, Wil asks in exasperation whether he is bound forever to his humble cottage, never rising above poverty, resents the fact that his wife Elin is trapped in a cage of grief, and fears that the Lord will provide them at most with enough to survive.

In *Y Pasg* (*Easter*) by J.R. Jones, the portraits of local people bring us into the realm of modernist writing. We meet Twm Rhos-lwyd, his cheeks round and red as two apples, the peak of his cap roofing his brow, and tobacco juice staining his jaw. Twm Rhos-Llwyd can set the scythe whistling through a hilly meadow, and, come harvest time, knows how to clap the stooks onto a ram's back. Then comes Rhys y Gaer, peering over his spectacles like a child over an orchard wall. Once he owned an estate, and until he spent his wealth in the ale-house, the sheen of his horses was proverbial in the land. In the work of J.R. Jones Tal-y-bont, memories of North Ceredigion in the early 20th century are sometimes tinged with a poignancy that is more than nostalgia. Come spring, and the first tourists and visitors, there are none of the old tribe left to observe their passage, he writes, just the splash of trout in 'Private Lakes', and the buzzard on its nest high up on the rock.

In the work of the rural poets of Ceredigion in the 20th century, descriptions of people's lives reach maturity in the work of W.J. Gruffydd and John Roderick Rees. In *Unigedd* (*Solitude*), W.J. Gruffydd produces enduring images, writing of old hands, red and raw with work, reaching for the saucepan by the gable to take some swill from the pig's tub, its bitter stench laced with turf-smoke and the smell of sweat from the mare's back.

A poem of the same title, *Unigedd* (*Solitude*) by John Roderick Rees is the saga of a girl of poor parents who leaves home young to work as a maid. First the poem sets the scene, describing the ruins of her childhood home, Pant-yr-Oen. There, the stone and peat of the mountainside form the body of the cottage's four walls. Song drowns there in the unrelenting drizzle, and, in winter, snow smiles lavishly on the bulrush and stagnant pools. Pant yr Oen is the place where Sara first saw the light of day clawing its way across y Gors Rydd, a leaden light as the January sun sank low.

Sara was another mouth in the crowded kitchen around the bare table, another mouth to feed with crumbs from the bog land, yet another who, when her time came, would walk down the overgrown path where the chill winds dispersed a people. We are told more about the circumstances of the family, of life's cruelty in the mud-cottage, of nights when little coffins were carried out under one arm, of children caught in the clutches of pox and tuberculosis and laid to sleep under a bone of mountain.

No other poem in the corpus tells us more about the lives of women in rural Ceredigion than *Solitude* by John Roderick Rees. We are introduced to Sara's mother, a woman small of frame, her arms fragile, who assumed her burden both when the chatter of young children brought cheer and when she craved for the earth and soil of her few acres. The narrative tells more of Sara and her life and how, a tender twelve years old, she crossed the threshold of the school door for the last time, accepted the small advance payment that was offered to servants at the time, and gathered up her ragged clothes, not forgetting to pack a Bible in the trunk, lest misfortune beset her on her way.

The world she finds herself in once she has taken her place in the big house is characterised by segregation, the two-tabled kitchen, house and byre, church and chapel, squire, land-holder and male servants, each tending to his own social niche while observing a requisite silence. Sara was still a child when, one bright chilly morning by the cow house where she would shovel out the dung and feed the animals, she wept her tears of solitude.

So her life continued for all of forty years, season to season, from one frugal year to the next, a life spent shuffling from one unfamiliar manor to the next before turning, old and stooping, to the seclusion of the hills. There Sara returns after forty years to the place where once the children played like a flock of swallows, but where now only generations of crickets in the hearth have survived the silence of the mud walls.

Returning home does not bring an end to solitude. On

her return to Pant-yr-Oen, Sara finds there is not a soul with whom to hold a simple conversation, only the occasional hiker shouldering his pack, roaming the high ground, his steps regular as the pendulum of a grandfather clock in a country kitchen.

ATGOFION CARDI
THOMAS RICHARDS

PART III
HORIZONS

Women in the Work of the Ceredigion Bards

Rural life in Wales before the mechanised era conforms to a model typical of many traditional, agrarian societies. The men drove the plough, shod the horses, and wielded the scythe, while the women carried water, tended the fire, and spun the cloth. The men provided the food, while the women prepared it. The men built the houses in which the women reared the children. The men made not only the artefacts necessary for agricultural work, but also the artefacts and implements necessary for the functioning of domestic life, including furniture, pots and pans, footwear and the wheels and carriages necessary for transport and haulage.

In other aspects of life, both men and women played their part. Here we note medicine and healing, for example, a domain that sometimes reaches into the realm of the occult in which women were influential. Funerary tasks and customs are also divided between men and women, though the division is clear: the men handle the coffin outside and beyond the house, while, within four walls, the women prepare the deceased for burial. Life in Wales, as elsewhere, was organised along these lines.

David Jenkins (p. 75) visits the theme of the division of labour: 'A basic feature of the customary organisation of farm work was its division into men's work and women's work. The men were responsible for the cultivation and the general labouring work of the farm while the women undertook the dairying and the work of the farmhouse and the farmyard. Correspondingly it took two people to run a farm, the master and the mistress, who were respectively the heads of each division of the work'. He adds (p. 75): 'These two roles were filled by the husband and the wife respectively where the farm was occupied by a married couple', and then continues: 'The mistress was responsible for the female staff, daughters and maids where there were both. She herself prepared the household's food and undertook the butter-making and the cheese-making, perhaps helped by one of the maids, but the greater part of the maids' time was occupied not in the farm-house but on the farm-yard'. Significantly, 'the maids did not work in the fields except during the harvests when they helped in loading the hay and at the ricks, and in binding the sheaves during the corn harvest'.

The following remarks by David Jenkins are also relevant: 'The dairying was the mistress's responsibility, and this was not confined to work in the dairy but included much of the care of the milk cattle. South-west Wales was known as an area where a high proportion of female labour was employed on farms. According to the *Third Report of the Committee on the Employment of Children etc. in Agriculture* (1870) 'in the ordinary routine of farm work, the women servants tend cattle, clean out the stables, load dung carts, plant and dig potatoes, hoe, take up, top and tail turnips, and in the spring drive the harrow, but they are never entrusted with horses and carts on the high road'.

Jenkins continues (p. 44) as follows, and here the phrase 'others who occupied cottages' is important in that it imposes the distinction between gender-specific work, and class-related work: 'Widows, spinsters and others who occupied cottages without land undertook the incidental tasks of the countryside. They knitted stockings, they were specialist makers of oatcakes, and visited farms to work in that capacity. They collected stones from the hayfields and placed them in roadside heaps to earn payment from the highways authority; some worked as quilt makers, as dressmakers, and others specialised in the trade of making women's garters. They were casual workers at farms where they were paid for an occasional day's washing or potato-sorting'.

From the dawn of our era, as early as the first quarter of the last millennium, production of wool is central to life in Wales. Along with tasks and responsibilities typical of women's lives in other cultures, women in Wales, due to the relative importance of wool, played a major part in spinning, knitting and selling woollen products, blankets and socks, for example. Making cloth, like other activities mentioned above, involves a measure of work that can be done by men or by women, either alone, in small groups by the members of one family, or collectively where a village comes together. And in each of these contexts, in many societies, lyric and narrative tradition become relevant. Over the centuries in Wales, song, poetry, legend and myth are at the heart of the culture. What roles did men and women respectively play in this area of life?

In the past, the bard in Wales belonged to a guild who spent part of the year travelling. Professional bards in medieval times travel from patron to patron, on horseback, accompanied by a servant perhaps. Journeying was not always safe, and a knowledge of the use of arms was advantageous. The bard travels alone or in semi-solitude in unprotected spaces, and crosses a territory that may be hostile. In traditional societies, women do not generally move in unprotected spaces, especially not alone. For reasons such as these, female activity, including the practice of poetry, will tend to take place either in the domestic environment or within the defined space of village or parish.

This seems to be reflected in the corpus of *hen benillion,* popular old rhymes that belong largely to the period from the 16th to the 18th century. In T.H. Parry Williams' collection of verse from this tradition, there are innumerable examples of female compositions. The editor writes: '[we find] lullabies, hunting songs, milking-songs and spinning-songs, songs for the oxen and so forth'.

In *Ar Gefn ei Geffyl* (*Man on Horse*) (Cymdeithas Lyfrau Ceredigion, 1969), writings on rural life in Ceredigion, author Richard Phillips includes a short chapter on *Alys Pantcoch – Prydyddes y Bryniau (Alys of Pantcoch – Poetess of the Hills)* (p. 29): 'She strove to write in verse events from the New Testament, and to describe the characteristics of Christian religion, and of the world around her'. In *Hen Ŷd y Wlad,* Isfoel devotes two pages to Crannogwen (1839–1916), the pen-name of an important figure in Dyfed in the 19th century whose name was Sarah Rees. She was, he says 'a poetess, preacher and social leader'. A collection of her verse, *Caniadau Crannogwen* (*The Songs of Crannogwen*), appeared in 1870, and she was editor from 1878–1916 of *Y Frythones,* a Welsh-language magazine for women. Eluned Phillips (1914–2009) of Cenarth, South Ceredigion, was a literary figure of some stature in Wales in her day, winning the crown at the National *Eisteddfod* twice, and frequenting in Paris the company of internationally renowned artists. A book of her work *Cerddi Glyn-y-Mêl* was published in 1985.

The female novelist and author of books for children, Maelona (1878–1953), a native of the Rhydlewis area in Southern Ceredigion, was one of the foremost writers of Welsh prose, male or female, in West Wales in the early 20th century. Her family saga tells of three generations from the farm *Ffynnonloyw,* of religious fervour, votes for women, education, and of the Anglicisation of South Wales.

Cassie Davies (1898–1988) of Tregaron was another well-known figure in Ceredigion and Wales in her day. Her literary talents were channelled into the traditional art of storytelling, the realm of the medieval *cyfarwydd* in Welsh culture. The tradition of contribution by women to literature in Ceredigion is carried on by Caryl Lewis (1978), whose novels *Martha Jac a Sianco* (2004) and *Y Gemydd* (*The Jeweller*) (2007) and *Y Bwthyn* (*The Cottage*) (2015) afford insights into rural life. In *Teulu'r Cilie* (*The Family of Cilie Farm*), Jon Merion Jones writes of Esther Jones (1886–1964), describing (p. 188) how she recited rhyme and verse, some perhaps composed extempore.

The idea of writing rhyme and verse down was not current in West Wales during the early part of our period. The tradition was a strongly oral one. In *Pen and Plough*, we present work by a number of poets born in the 19th century including Isfoel, Isgarn, Evan Rowlands, B.T. Hopkins and Alun Cilie. Like their sisters, none sang or wrote with a view to publishing. Both Isfoel and B.T. Hopkins were almost 80 when a collection of their work appeared. Alun Cilie was in his late 60s when persuaded to publish. The work of Isgarn and Evan Rowlands was published posthumously. In several ways, each of these bards, born before 1900, continue to function in the same way in the 20th century as did their peers, both male and female, in the 19th century. In the case of the women poets, for want perhaps of a champion of their work, their work was not collected and made available in book form.

Importantly, changes in work-patterns, and mechanisation of work, affects the environment with which a particular type of verse was associated. With the advent of the industrial woollen mills therefore, the spinning-song no longer had a stage. Ploughing songs sung to entice the oxen were already archaic before our period, surviving deep into the nineteenth century only in Glamorganshire, it seems. Also, due in part to the temperance movement, and to the religious revival of 1904-05, hymn-singing grew in popularity, and other forms of expression fell silent, including 'pieces' sung and composed by women, songs of love and courtship, for example.

However, during the 1904–05 revival, the traditional order of things was revised, at least in the context of the prayer meetings. David Jenkins writes (pp 231-232): 'One of the features of the revival was that it upset or reversed the roles of different members of the congregation: the young people commonly took over the meetings, women became extremely prominent...' He then continues (p. 233): 'Many [women] became national figures [during the revival], known for their testimonies and as 'gospel singers', and 'at Cardigan the women established their own prayer meetings, and these, so we read in the Cardigan and Tivy-Side Advertiser (9 Dec. 1904) 'increased Sunday by Sunday without being announced, it being an entirely spontaneous movement on their part'.

Returning to the simple observation that, in a traditional society, house and hearth constitute the domain of the woman, while the men direct their work toward the field, we are now in a position to make observations that help us interpret the body of work in hand. The literary tradition in Wales is strongly oral, includes verse, song and storytelling, and is practiced by both man and women. In the present study, however, we are confined to interpreting the work of male poets for two principal reasons: our central theme is expression of man's relationship with the earth, and our source is verse published in book form in the second half of the 20th century where major changes in this relationship are documented. Our Ceredigion poets do not write about domestic matters. It is not a provocation to observe that, in their verse, their wives and children are given less attention than their dogs and horses. This state of affairs is not a reflection of their lives or personal convictions. It is a reflection of the things that fall into their remit as wordsmiths, craftsmen and farmers.

There are exceptions. Elegies for deceased children form a sub-corpus in the work of the bards from medieval times. This tradition continues, or is renewed, in the 20th century, and in *Galarnad* (*Elegy*), written for his daughter Esyllt who died a child, Dic Jones equals or surpasses all former exponents of the genre with lines such as '*ei dawn i wylo yw gwerth dynoliaeth*', 'man's merit is his ability to mourn' (*Sgubo'r Storws,* p. 31). Here we note, however, that while suffering and sentiment are indeed expressed by the poet, this is not done within the domestic space. In the context of his child's heart-rending death, the poet alludes to no place other than the hospital at Glangwili, Carmarthen. Here too, the line is utterly disarming: '*Glyn galar fydd Glangwili*', he writes in *cynghanedd,* 'Glangwili [hospital] shall remain for me a vale of tears'.

Interestingly, the women we are introduced to in the poetry of Ceredigion in the 20th century tend, as a rule, to be outside their domestic quarters. Isfoel's *Nani Ffebi* (*Ail Gerddi,* p. 65), 'a simple and vigorous old girl', goes visiting, knitting as she walks. In *Yr Helfa* (*The Quest*) (pp 37-39), Isgarn writes of a female figure, Ann Lena, gathering berries. Both these women seem to be beyond child-bearing age, and are certainly portrayed in an asexual way. So too is seventy-year-old *Ellen Ann* (*Agor Grwn,* p. 40) in a poem of that title by Dic Jones.

Occasional poems refer light-heartedly to courtship or marriage. *Y Mis Mêl* (*Honeymoon*) by Isfoel (*Ail Gerddi* Isfoel, p. 49) is a good example. The couple drive to Anglesey, have their photograph taken, and conclude that, should they have a daughter, they will name her Menai, after the straits between the mainland and the island. *Y Carwr Swil* (*The Bashful Lover*), a long poem by Isfoel (*Ail Gerddi*, pp 77-79), illustrates well the humorous vein in which love and courtship is often presented. The poor lad in question, Wil, goes to pieces when Ann comes to see him at a late hour, and takes her handkerchief to hide his blushing cheeks.

In *I'm Hanwylyd* (*For My Loved One*) (*Cerddi*, pp 138-139), John Roderick Rees undertakes to express his sentiments. He seems less at home with this theme, however, than with themes related to the land, for example, and the poem, while sincere, remains somewhat pedestrian. 'I cannot explain the depth of my love for you,' he tells his loved one. Other work by John Roderick Rees however is outstanding in any context in its portrayal of the reality of women's lives. The first of the two examples that come to mind is *Unigedd* (*Solitude*).

The second poem in which John Roderick Rees writes at length about an individual woman is called *Glannau*, a nine-page poem that describes several years of dementia endured by his foster-mother, during which time the poet nursed her. He likens his foster-mother to a vessel thrown onto the high seas soon after she turned seventy, noting that a narrow sound opened up between them, widening each day. As the poem nears a conclusion the poet states: 'I shall strive to stretch a hand across the sea'.

J.M. Edwards is another poet who succeeds in dealing with sentiment and emotion in a way untypical of rural Welsh tradition. His *Marwnad ym Mehefin* (*Lament in June*), for example, is full of poise, dignity, and lyric skill. Few poems in Welsh in the 20th century can match the imagination and originality of his letter from Héloïse to Abélard, inspired by the tragic medieval love-story of

Héloïse d'Argenteuil and philosopher Pierre Abélard. J.M. Edward's *Héloïse to Abélard* is discussed in *Beyond the Horizon* in Part IV of this book. The poem includes the only reference to physical love that I am aware of in the whole corpus. Héloïse receives a letter written, she reflects, by a hand that once possessed her utterly, a hand that once caressed her breasts, and knew each intimate contour of her body.

In general, and in contrast to this, women are addressed in tones formal or restrained, in birthday greeting, for example, or on other occasions when the poet chooses to congratulate a female member of the community. We cite one example, *Yn Gant Oed* (*One Hundred Years Old*), a poem by John Roderick Rees (*Cerddi Newydd / New Poems*, pp 75-76) for a certain Mrs Margaret Jones of Penuwch. Mrs Jones, he writes, cultivated throughout the years, a certain noble dignity, and walked as a queen amongst her people. The books of the Ceredigion bards in the 20th century contain countless verses where reference to members of the community, men and women, remains formal and stylised. They continue the tradition of eulogy and elegy that characterises the work of the Welsh bards in other ages.

ar
ymylon
cors
caron
EVAN
JONES

Mining and Miners

In Wales, mining is often associated with the coal-pits of the Glamorganshire Valleys where the growth of the industry revolutionised national life and shaped the economy of the country. In the deceptive quiet of the West, Ceredigion has its own history of mining too, not coal, but zinc, lead and silver, for example. It is a history long and rich: centuries before the Romans exploited the ore deposits of the county, earlier cultures were active in the extraction of these precious resources. In the post-medieval period, mining recommenced, and by the nineteenth century the mountains of Ceredigion were a hive of mining activity. Large populations grew up around the mining sites in the Rheidol Valley, in Gogerddan and in Cwmsymlog some miles further north, and in Tal-y-bont nearby. But of all the places in Ceredigion where mining became a central part of local life, none is better known for its literary culture than the village of Ffair Rhos.

W. Jones-Edwards describes the village as follows in his 'autobiography of a miner', a book entitled *Ar Lethrau Ffair Rhos* (*On the Hillsides of Ffair Rhos*) (Cymdeithas Lyfrau Ceredigion, 1963): 'Ffair Rhos is a small village in the Ceredigion midlands close to the border with Radnorshire [Welsh 'Sir Faesyfed']. It stands about a mile from the village of Pontrhydfendigaid, or 'Y Bont' as it is commonly known in its abbreviated form. Nearby too is the Monastery of Strata Florida, a romantic and tranquil spot where the remains of abbots, monks and princes lie alongside the dead of many generations of parishioners, and the bones of [the famous bard] Dafydd ap Gwilym' who lived in the early to mid-14th century.

In his book, the old miner tells a little of the history of the place name *Ffair Rhos*: 'We can state with confidence that some of the most important fairs in Ceredigion were held here in days gone by. This helps explain the name *Ffair Rhos*. It is said the fairs were begun originally to sell the wool of the sheep of Strata Florida Monastery.' In a lengthy ballad entitled *Y Ffair* (*The Fair*), local bard Evan Jenkins (1895–1959) describes in vivid detail his early memories of a big fair in the village. The piece is published in *Cerddi Ffair Rhos* (1959), a collection of poems and ballads. He describes how, on the 25th of September, the fair was held each year, but that by his time it had become obsolete. The fair, as well as being a hub of trade, was associated with entertainment, and with drinking. As a result, fighting at fairs was common in Wales in the late 19th century. In a short essay published in 1943 called *Ffair y Borth* (*The Fair of Porthaethwy*), Sir Ifor Williams describes the scenes at the fair as related to him by a then 85-year-old native of the village of Porthaethwy, a certain Mr Owen Hughes. The essay forms part of a posthumous collection published in 1968 and entitled *Meddai Syr Ifor* (*Thus Spoke Sir Ifor*): 'His [Owen Hughes'] earliest memory of the Fair, when he was an eight-year old boy, in 1867 or thereabouts, was seeing men fighting with each other at the Cross in the middle of Porthaethwy; men stripped off to the waist. But there was more than just the use of the fists, punching and kicking mercilessly and making a terrible mess of each other.'

These recollections of a man born in the mid-19th century in North Wales concur with what W. Jones-Edwards has to say in *Ar Lethrau Ffair Rhos* (*On the Slopes of Ffair Rhos*): 'The fiercest fighting of all would take place in Pontrhydfendigaid on the evening of Ffair Gŵyl y Grog, Holy Rood Day, on the 25th of September. Before the fair, the publicans would take all the crockery upstairs and put planks around the furniture in case they might be smashed to pieces.'

There was more to a fair than fighting, and, as Evan Jenkins' poem reminds us, the fair attracted different kinds of people, making it an exotic occasion for the crofter and miner and their families. He describes amongst others the gypsies who would come in their caravans, early at break of day, with their children and skinny greyhounds, and their weary old horses who were glad to be freed of their harness. The fair over, all returned to homes described as follows by W. Jones-Edwards (ibid, p.4): 'Most of the miners lived in small-holdings with between ten to fifteen acres of land. These had probably been *one-night* houses originally...The houses had one chimney, and were thatched with rushes...The floors were of earth, or flagstones.'

He then makes these remarks (ibid, p. 9): 'Without whatever land formed part of the small-holding of a miner, the family table would have been extremely bare. Most kept two cows and a horse, fattened a calf and usually two pigs. Some had a small number of sheep as well'. The following insight into the social structure of the mining village enhances the context of poems that we shall introduce presently. W. Jones-Edwards writes (ibid, p. 14): 'The habitants [of Ffair Rhos] could be divided roughly into three classes. The upper class was formed of members of the Church. As a rule, these were farmers. The middle class was formed of Methodists, farmers some, or traders. The lower class was made up of miners, farm-hands and those who worked on the roads. Most of these were Baptists.'

In *Llwch* (*Dust*) by John Roderick Rees, the poet encapsulates the history of migration from rural Ceredigion to the industrial South. He addresses a young crofter, and talks to him of his father who moves to the dusty Rhondda to escape a hungry life and the tether of fruitless crofting on a bare acre of peatland. In its six parts, the poem *Llwch* (*Dust*) describes the conditions in which the workers spent their week. Here, the particles of dust sing their song of death, bedevilling the miners' lungs, where they make their nest. There is no ointment in a tin that can ever rid the affected lung of the stain.

The spectacle of the menfolk leaving Ffair Rhos to seek work in the South is described by W. Jones-Edwards (ibid, p. 52): 'The morning of the 'departure', mother and children would be about the house at an early hour, and once the cart disappeared from Ffair Rhos, they would go to the top of one of the little hills to see the train pull out of Strata [Florida]. Eyes welling up with tears, they would peer at the smoke until the train passed Alltddu and disappeared on its way to Tregaron.'

In another passage, however, he makes the point that life was better in the South. Home for a visit, the men would speak as follows in praise of their new environment (ibid, p. 53-54): 'The streets are paved. No walking through the puddles there. The streets are lit all night long. Plenty of cinemas where a man can have a bit of fun. And if you haven't made dinner, all you have to do is send the kids to Brachi's to get some fish and chips...Yeah, we're just mugs hanging around a kip like this.'

Direct reference to the mines of Ceredigion is to be found in the work of several poets. For example, in *Yr Arloeswr* (*The Pioneer*) by Dafydd Jones, we read how he recalls the pit-horns before they fell silent. He recalls also the miners, scarred by toil, who pieced the land together on the steep, open slopes to create their small farms.

In the work of J.R. Jones, the mining community is mentioned in *Y Groesffordd* (*The Crossroads*) in the collection *Rhwng Cyrn yr Aradr* (*Driving the Plough*). He describes them as a merry band, adding that once they enjoyed coming to the crossroads when they had earned brief respite from their labour. They never had either riches or comfort, and their lot was to dig out a feast for their idle masters.

In another poem by J.R. Jones, *Ymson y Mynydd* (*The Mountain Speaks*), the poet describes the miners as mere thralls on the altar of plenty who knew what it was to bend their backs for a wage that was no more than a pittance. Coughing into the soil, they could hope only for the solace of an early grave.

Despite the hardship of their lives, we are reminded in W. Jones-Edwards' autobiography of another aspect of the culture, and of the intellectual life in which many of the miners participated (p. 39): 'This [small room where the miners rested] was the focal point of discussions about all kinds of subjects – political, religious, theological, and local.' And he refers directly to the importance of poetry in proletariat culture in Ceredigion in the early 20th century: 'How many *englyn, telyneg* and *pryddest* were composed in these underground pits?' he says, referring to three of the metres and forms practiced at the time.

Ffenestri (*Windows*) by W.J. Grufffydd is the source of the following words where the human face of the miners of Ffair Rhos is evident. We note that the collection is dedicated to 'the miners of Esgair Mwyn' and to the inhabitants of 'Llanfihangel-Eisiau-Bwyd', an ironic toponym coined by the author that we might translate as 'The Hungry Parish of St Michael'. We meet the head of the household who steps across the raised wooden threshold at cock crow, already pressed for time despite the early hour. The frost is sharp, and it scalds the skin, recalling the water used to singe the pig's skin on slaughtering day. The man ventures over the bog to Esgair Mwyn to join the cohort of ashen-faced shapes who spit dust from their lungs. W.J. Gruffydd continues to say that these bearded young men are destined to have grown old before their young are raised, and before the bills have been settled in the village shop.

Few poems in the corpus of work bequeathed to us by the poets of Ceredigion in the 20th century are as poignant in a private way as *Esgair Mwyn*, a place name in Ffair Rhos that might be translated literally as the 'mineral ridge'. Here W.J. Gruffydd speaks of his father and grandfather, miners both in their day. The remnants of their years of bondage lie in the depths of the pit underneath the stagnant waters. On a ledge somewhere in the mine, he surmised that some of the tallow from their faint candles is most probably still be found, candles that burned for them in the darkest of days. Another of the six quatrains of the poem *Esgair Mwyn* describes the dual existence of the farmer-miner. In spring, the men followed the single-furrow plough over their crusty land. To supplement their income, they searched for bread, and found it, between the gaping jaws of the mine, sweating their souls out until Sunday brought the blessing of brief rest.

The last of the mines of Ceredigion closed in the early 20th century. Woodland has reclaimed some of the sites. Others still evoke their heyday; Cwmsymlog, for example, where debris covers the face of the valley.

HENRI MENDRAS
LA FIN DES PAYSANS
BABEL
ESSAI

The Sea

Poems in Welsh about the sea occur very infrequently in the literary tradition from medieval to modern times. There is no great classical poem from either era it seems, inspired by the depths of the ocean, the fury of the storm, the seemingly infinite expanse of tide and wave. Welsh bards, on the whole, did not consider themselves sailors. In a 14th century poem by Gruffydd Gryg, *I'r Lleuad* (*To the Moon*) (*The Oxford Book of Welsh Verse* p. 94-96), the poet finds himself on board a ship in the Bay of Biscay on his way to St Jacques de Compostella. He blames the moon for raising the wind and sea to a storm, making his journey a misery, but hardly mentions the sea at all.

Other bards of the 14th to 16th centuries, whether Dafydd ap Gwilym, Lewis Glyn Cothi, Tudur Aled or others, make occasional reference to their horses, harps, servants, to their patrons, to the church, to the woods and rivers, and to their lovers, real or imagined. More than a passing reference to the sea is unusual, and its waters are often seen as hostile. Thus, in the poem *Y Don ar Afon Dyfi* (*The Wave on the River Dyfi*), Dafydd ap Gwilym pleads with the tide to let him cross from the North into Ceredigion so that he may hasten to his loved one.

In Ceredigion in the 20th century, this state of affairs is largely reflected, and the land-orientated nature of the tradition is resoundingly confirmed. However, we do find a wonderful exception to the rule. In a long poem by Samuel Bartholomew Jones (1894–1964), one of the Cilie Family, we read in detail the voyage of one of the last sailing ships in the early 20th century to sail *Around the Horn*. The poem can take its place not only in the recent Ceredigion tradition, but in Welsh tradition as a whole as an expression in rolling, native Welsh of the wonders of the sea.

In a comprehensive book, *Morwyr y Cilie* (*The Seamen of the Cilie Family*), Jon Meirion Jones documents the relationship of members of the Cilie family of South Ceredigion with the sea and with the shipping industry. He writes as follows of S.B. Jones: 'S.B. was the only one of the second generation of the Cilie Family who went to sea. Though he spent less time at sea than any of the other eight members of the third generation, it might be said on the other hand that he is the most famous of the seamen of Cilie. The reason for this is the fact that he wrote *Round the Horn*, winning the National *Eisteddfod* in Wrexham in 1933.'

S.B. Jones takes his imagery from the world of the plough as he leaves the shelter of the port. The bright sunlight is glinting on his plough at home in Wales, where on the cliffs the blade is now disused and rusting. He gleans further images from the world of the farmer to describe the sea as he observes the ridges of the grey green acres of the Channel and the cross-ridge of the horizon receding through wind and rain.

The description of the sailors at work is vivid. 'Furl the royals!' The order rings out, and in no time at all there are six sailors aloft on the rigging, S.B. Jones among them. They climb up crow-legged on the mast, as if on a bare tree in winter. Welshman Jones then finds himself with Irish Mac undoing and tying rope after rope high above the deck. These lines are unique in the Welsh tradition. Much more in keeping with the love of terra firma are the following musings by Alun Cilie, S.B. Jones' younger brother. In *Y Bae* (*The Bay*) Alun first admits his fascination for the many moods of the sea, stating his love for the sea's broad acres, while, like his brother S.B. turning to the land for his imagery. The poet loves the sea's blue-green wave, its passionate song, its roar, its smile, and the shine of its curving blade, its throaty growl amidst the towering rocks, and its loud outbursts in the caves. Finally, he is enthralled by the terrible boiling wrath of its white horses as they dash forth to break on the rocks.

Unlike his brother S.B., however, Alun says that he was never sufficiently drawn by the sea's charms to marry her and become a sailor. The longing to sail the sea's unfenced lea was never greater than his desire to remain on the land. He tells of the old seamen whose company he enjoyed, and their fresh store of witty tales. Untroubled and resourceful men they were, he says, sipping beer and recalling all they had been through.

The old seamen Alun Cilie refers to are men he would have met as a boy in or near Cardigan town and port. In the early 1800s, over 300 sailing ships and a thousand sea-farers were registered in Cardigan, and the town enjoyed a boom in ship-building. Slate from Dol Badau three miles upstream on the River Teifi was exported through the harbour, as was wood from the forests, while trade in herring and salmon was brisk in season. Soon however, the estuary began to silt up, limiting access, and with the arrival of the train in the Teifi Valley and its hinterland in the 1880s, the port entered a period of decline that was never reversed. In *The Bay,* Alun Cilie documents this decline, commenting on the abandoned harbour and the lonely quay. The good steel moorings that once held all the immense force of a ship heaving in the swell, they too stood idle. The warehouse on the banks of the River Teifi has in recent years been renovated. In Alun Cilie's time and in the poem *The Bay* however, they paint a picture of dejection. One building stands on a fist of beach, dilapidated, doorless, emptied of its treasures, and soul-less.

In North Ceredigion, between Aberystwyth and Aberdyfi, the tradition seems to remain silent on the subject of shipping and seafaring. J.R. Jones of Tal-y-bont is at home in the mountain, and refers to the shores of his native county only briefly and in the context of tourism and holidays. In the poem *Ymwelwyr* (*Visitors*) for example, he writes how pleasant it is to go rambling in Ynyslas, or clamber over the rocks in Borth. How pleasant to meet there people of other races and cultures. How pleasant to experience this paradise before returning to the ant-hill cities and the dust of the coal-mining valleys.

In another text, a light-hearted ballad called *Siôn Glan-Don* (*Siôn By-the-Wave*), he tells of a local character living in a hut on the shore away from the rest of society. All feared the worst for *Siôn Glan-Don* on stormy nights when the sea and wind raged, but efforts to persuade him to move from the humble shelter fell on deaf ears. The pilgrim would not be moved. And so it came it pass: one morning the shelter had disappeared, and with it forever *Siôn Glan-Don*.

The Cilie family remain the strongest link in Ceredigion between the land and the sea. In the 1980s, while visiting Llangrannog and Pontgarreg, I found the atmosphere in some of the local houses to be quite unique. Everything spoke of the land, the community, of a palpable order of the kind reflected and nurtured in the poetry. Here too the rich sonority of the Welsh language was sovereign. On the kitchen wall however hung pictures of ships and ship-captains, not of Welsh Cob and prize ribbons, as in the kitchen of John Roderick Rees some forty miles away on the mountain near Tregaron.

The attraction of the sea for S.B. Jones and others of the extended family is explained by the fact that much of the land of the Cilie Farm runs along the cliffs above the swell below. In a short foreword to Alun Cilie's first volume of poems (1964), D.J. Roberts writes as follows: 'There is hardly another farmhouse in South Ceredigion as remote as Y Cilie. There would be much truth in saying that it is easier to reach Y Cilie by sea than by land, because nearby lies the famous Cilie Beach.' D.J. Roberts continues: '[Cilie Beach] was home to the smugglers many years ago, but by now the place has been discovered by the wealthy inhabitants of our cities, and Cilie, amidst the noise of all the motorcars is not as difficult to reach as it used to be.'

A short passage from S.B. Jones' *Around the Horn,* so evocative of a maritime world in its last years, seems the most fitting way to conclude this chapter. Reference to the *Tripolia,* the boat on which S.B. Jones sailed will be of interest to historians of maritime culture, and the pride of the last of the true sailors in an age of steam shines through the writing. Irish, Welsh and German; all work together with rope and sail short years before the Great War drove nations on a course of mutual annihilation. The *Tripolia* groans, writes S.B. Jones of Cilie Farm, listing heavily in the turbulence. Only the topsails are unfurled and the deck rises up in the waves like the gable-end of a house. His fellow seaman, a certain Fritz, declares he would like to show the strength of his beam to the 'velvet' sailors whose new ships are driven not by the wind, but by steam.

HEN ŶD
Y WLAD
ISFOEL

Immigration into Ceredigion

Before 1970, there is no discussion in the work of the rural poets of Ceredigion of immigration or of linguistic diversity. This is an accurate reflection of the demography of West Wales at the time. Apart from an occasional doctor, academic or refugee, the society was homogenously Welsh, and homogenously Welsh-speaking, as it had been for centuries. Certain members of this society had already acquired proficiency in English by the beginning of our period, the 1880s, but, on the other hand, monoglot speakers were still to be found in the county until the end of the 20th century. Significantly, the demise of the culture of the big houses in the late 19th century, and their extinction in the early 20th century, retarded the advance of English in the rural West. During the first quarter of the 20th century therefore, before the age of the car, and before people began to listen regularly to the 'wireless', the countryside was as Welsh-speaking as it had been at any time in history.

The first reference to change is to be found in *Cerddi J.R. Jones* (1970). A native of Cwm Eleri near Tal-y-bont north of Aberystwyth, J.R. Jones witnessed the development of the tourist industry in his area. Tourism as such is distinct from resettlement, and involves principally seasonal traffic. However, a fortnight's holiday in Wales was a step towards the purchase of summer houses and permanent homes by outsiders, this in turn leading to residency in Wales of an increasing number of incomers.

Two poems on this theme occur in *Cerddi J.R. Jones* (*The Poems of J.R. Jones*). The first is called *Ymwelwyr* (*Visitors*). It speaks of summer arriving in a splash to paint hill and meadow, and to hand each tree its finest parasol. He addresses the visitors, saying he knows they too will come to seek the clean air. Come they will, both from the hubbub of the city, and from the black dust of the coal-mining valleys.

In the second poem, *Craig y Felin* (*Mill Rock*), the incomers have begun to establish themselves, spending their time now in holiday bungalows. J.R. Jones notes in *Craig y Felin* the pretty bungalows nestled together in the sunshine under a veranda of trees. No factory smoke reaches them there, and there is no sound of heavy vehicles to disturb the peace of their quiet homes in the valley.

The tourists stay a while, but, significantly, soon leave when summer ends. In the last verse of *Craig y Felin* we read how the children lose their initial shyness, their gleeful voices then ringing out and filling the place with singing until autumn sounds its horn and plucks each leaf from the tree leaving both Craig y Felin and its little bungalows cloaked in silence.

Following the chronological order of books published by rural Ceredigion poets, the next references we find to change are in the work of B.T. Hopkins in whose book *Rhos Helyg a Cherddi Eraill* (*Rhos Helyg and Other Poems*) (1976), we find two poems on this theme, *Tyddyn y Gors* (*Moorland Croft*) and *Ein Tir* (*Our Land*). The first is an *englyn*, a four-line verse in strict metre. He notes that the Englishman thinks nothing of spending thousands of pounds to pay for a modest and remote dwelling. This, however, is the price of impoverishment, not of enrichment for Wales. For B.T. Hopkins, the coming of these first English settlers is a form of foreign infiltration.

Ein Tir (*Our Land*) contains five three-line verses. Two describe the environment in lyric and pastoral tones. B.T. Hopkins speaks of Ceredigion as a pocket of foaming rivers with its meadows, moors and woodlands. The Protestant work-ethic that characterises aspects of Welsh culture finds its way into the poet's lines, and he speaks of a land of industrious hands working the acres to produce hay and crops. A shadow is then cast on the page, and the poet asks despairingly whether the lovely earth shall be given up in waste to the stranger. Hopkins holds the strangers in contempt, calling them frail idlers, unlettered too, people without as much as a barn to their name. He concludes the poem *Our Land* in similar fashion, now describing the English settlers as being landless and subservient, and asking scathingly what virtue, if any, a rootless tree can take pride in.

Views such as this of the culture of the non-Welsh are not confined to the work of B.T. Hopkins. The poem *Cenhadwr Mamon* (*Mammon's Ambassador*) by J.R. Jones offers a caustic view of popular British culture. He portrays an ambient newspaper merchant, most probably in Aberystwyth, who, after a boozy night, pushes his cart to an empty station corner early on Sunday morning. The merchant lights a cigarette, and without raising his hand or voice, the people flock to buy the cheap evangel of the English. Finally, the poet passes judgement on the contents of the newspaper, a chronicle of ball and bookie where acts of scandals are mixed together with politics that is rotten to the core.

Cerddi Cwm Eleri (*Poems from Cwm Eleri*) (1980) is the title of J.R. Jones' third and final volume of poems. The writing in this collection may have lost much of the timbre and urgency of his early work, but it is an important source of information on matters economic, social, and ethnographic in North Ceredigion. Three poems from this collection discuss the theme of immigration; *Y Cwm* (*The Valley*), *Cymdogion* (*Neighbours*), and *Cyffes Hen Ffarmwr* (*Confession of an Old Farmer*).

The first, *Y Cwm* (*The Valley*), a four-page text, evokes life at various times in history. The poet is confident that life in the valley will continue as before, and writes quite simply that nobody can possibly become English in Cwm Eleri. The tone of *Cymdogion* (*Neighbours*) is, however, ironic and sarcastic. Change has occurred, but the poet brushes it off. He thanks the neighbours who give generously and bring modern society to Wales where once there only were lowly crofts. Thanks to their energy and wealth, he quips, the rural world has been revitalised.

Confession of an Old Farmer (ibid, p. 54) voices tensions that often remain private. The farmer states that his land is poor and his life hard. Rent gleaned in summer from tourists boosts his income. What better place to camp, he asks, that the green acre near his house? He turns the August sun to his advantage, and summer pays the rent. Caravans take the place of cow and calf.

Of all the poems in our extensive corpus, *Llygaid* (*Eyes*) by John Roderick Rees in *Cerddi Newydd* (*New Poems*) contains the most thorough expression of emotion and opinion regarding the influx into Ceredigion and West Wales of people from beyond the border. First the scene is set. The old farmhouse stands empty, but soon there are new occupants. We meet John Smith, described as being neighbourly, neat, and dispassionate. Language is the only wall that separates the poet from him. Next comes John Brown, solitary and inoffensive, who raises a hand in greeting from the shell of his car. A pekingese dog, perhaps his sole companion, sits by him, bobbing by on its seat. Other lines from *Llygaid* (*Eyes*) by John Roderick Rees are somewhat harsher. He describes the immigrants as being simply pig-ignorant, and brings them to task for spreading their muck over comely old holdings. His anger is unfettered when he accuses them of murdering the soil.

This poem was published in 1992, by which time immigration was beginning to change the face of society in Ceredigion. However, John Roderick Rees also writes words of welcome. Without the incomers, he says, there would be nothing in Penuwch and Bethania but the scrap-heap of the older families. But now, there are foreign hands working wool and leather, baking bread, putting a new sole on a shoe, and making clogs. The conviction that these things, if not good, are better than having no human culture at all on the mountain, is weaker however than the despair and anger the poet feels on seeing the change occur before his eyes. Amongst the new neighbours there are the bearded and the filthy, some living in makeshift camps, some lazily milking the Welfare State.

The Norman conquest of Southern Britain in the 12th century resulted in political change rather than in demographic change. The closure of the monasteries by Henry 8th in 1536 had far-reaching cultural consequences. However, it was not accompanied by mass immigration. Now, in the final decades of the 20th, the rural poets of Ceredigion, B.T. Hopkins, J.R. Jones, and John Roderick Rees, bear witness to the largest movement of people into Ceredigion since the time of the Roman Empire. The John Browns and John Smiths we meet in *Eyes* by John Roderick Rees are part of a movement of people that threatens Welsh, a language almost two millennia old, in the very heartland of its existence.

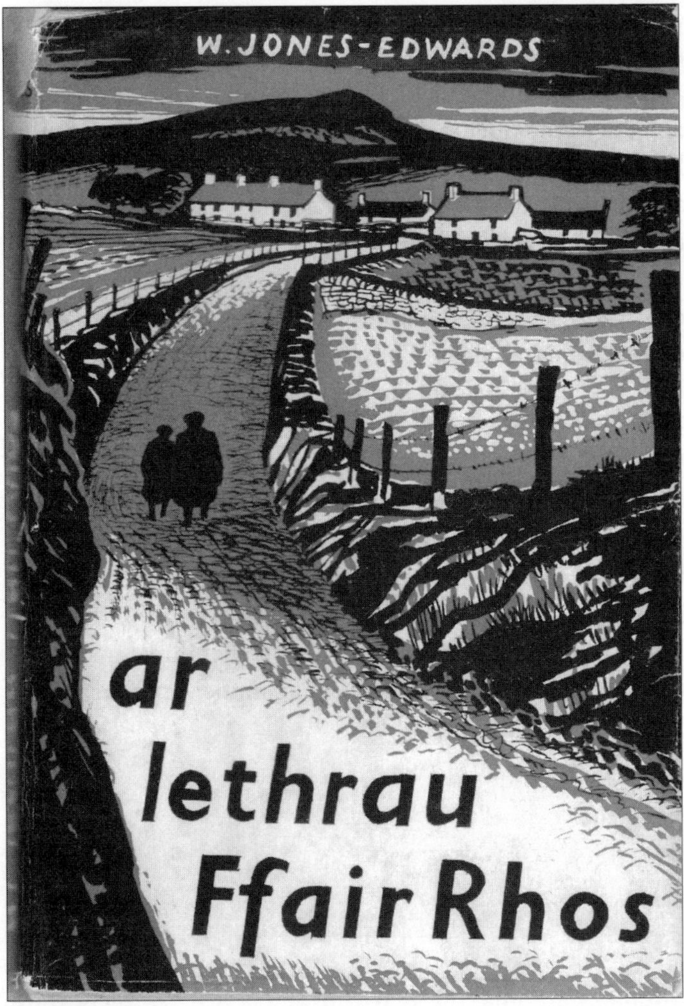
W. JONES-EDWARDS
ar
lethrau
Ffair Rhos

PART IV

INDIVIDUAL VOICES

A Poet and his Environment: J.R. Jones (1923–2002) Tal-y-bont, North Ceredigion

Seven miles north of Aberystwyth lies Tal-y-bont. In the late nineteenth century, the town was a thriving hub, its prosperity derived from the mining industry in the nearby hills. Just east of Tal-y-bont, in Cwm Eleri, J.R. Jones spent his life, farming the land, and composing verse. His work documents social and economic changes that include the demise of the local hill-farming communities, memories of the ore-mines of north Ceredigion, and the building of the Nant-y-Moch reservoir to supply electricity to Aberystwyth. The injustices of the landlord linger too in his work. Other themes that recur are the rise of the tourist industry, and the gradual suburbanisation of rural life. The work is bound together by a sense of man's relationship with a well-defined environment, and the tension in the work stems from change within this environment.

Social history in recent centuries in Wales may be viewed as a process defined by migration from mountainous land towards the river valleys, and vice versa, and by the dynamic created by this migration. Whereas at times in history, seasonal migration from *hendre* to *hafod*, from winter quarters to summer quarters, was a feature of Welsh culture, this semi-nomadic feature of the culture seems latterly to lead to polarisation whereby higher ground is exploited not only for its pastures, but also for the purpose of tillage on a small scale.

This is described in the three-part text *Cymell, Mentro, Llwyddo* (*Incitement, Venture, Prevail*). In *Incitement*, the poet writes how, on a brow of mountain, a walled enclosure was erected to shelter the ewe as she bore her first lamb, an enclosure whose rocks stood fast against the onslaught of the storms. The poet tells of the secluded nature of the old holding and how the intrepid pioneer is moved to prepare the soil for the seed, spreading lime when the season comes over the crusted earth.

Human settlement thereby becomes established on higher ground formerly uninhabited in winter, and contact with communities occupying the low-lying land – *llawr gwlad* – becomes confined to commercial exchanges on a seasonal basis. In the poem *Y Groesffordd* (*The Crossroads*), for example, we meet the smallholder who makes his way to join in the loud banter in the valley when fair-time comes around. The talk there will invariably be of deflated prices before the men return home to the peace of their frugal dwellings, replacing tracts of fern with soil fit for crops.

Moving on to the theme of the suburbanisation of rural life, J.R. Jones continually revisits the rural world he knew as a young man, and the characters who peopled that world. The poem *Yr Hen Bont* (*The Old Bridge*) from his first volume provides the setting. Among those crossing the bridge we find wise men for whom husbandry was a way of life. The poet describes them as being clad in homespun cloth as they return home from the feast of thanksgiving. Others too cross the bridge, bashful couples who hesitate before stealing past watchful eyes and enduring their jibes. But time continues to pass, and the mirth and cheer of yesteryear has expired. The poem records a custom practiced in the village when the crowd would take its weekly stroll, pausing to wind the village clock. Their laughter would fill the valley as they leaned back on the bridge wall before returning to their peat-fires higher up the valley.

During the lifetime of J.R. Jones, the stability of the existence of the small hill-farming community is undermined for several reasons, a phenomenon that underpins his work. One of these reasons is the development of transport and infrastructure. For the first time, visitors could now visit the countryside for a day. This increased mobility informs the poem *Tan y Graig,* a place-name meaning *By the Rock.* The poet mocks the day-trippers who seek serenity from the idle pleasures of their plastic world. They know nothing of the unfragmented contentment that the mountain has to offer. As the poem unfolds, the poet's emotions are heightened. The day-trippers seem to J.R. Jones be little more than noisy, agitated children coming and going in haste and commotion, their nerves cracking under the strain.

The imminent changes in the environment come as an added layer to other recent periods of change in the history of north Ceredigion. Short years before J.R. Jones came into the world, mining activity in the area ceased. In the 19th century, this mining industry was one factor that contributed to the sustainability of the mountain croft or small holding. Large communities grew up around several sites in Ceredigion including Cwmsymlog, Ystrad Einion, Goginan and Ffair Rhos. By J.R. Jones' time, these mines had all closed, but in the second quarter of the 20th century they still belong to a recent past. A poem in three parts, *Ymson y Mynydd* (*The Mountain Speaks*), begins with a description of mining life. Here the men heaved and grunted as they wielded pick and hammer. They worked by the light of rush candles to feed the avarice of the stranger. The day of the miner soon passed however, and none remain to honour their memory. The only evidence of their toil are criss-cross scars on the side of the mountain, and an occasional stone that bears the marks of their tools.

Although the past does provoke some nostalgia, the vibrant rural society depicted by J.R. Jones in his work may be said to have enjoyed stability for little more than a half a century between a time about 1900 when the hold of the lord on land and tenant was being loosened, until, at the very latest, 1960 when work began on an ambitious electrical plant in the Rheidol Valley and the water reservoir in the mountains at Nant-y-Moch between Tal-y-bont and Ponterwyd. This project and its consequences are described in a series of *englynion* entitled *Nant-y-Moch.* The poem begins by stating that a unique place has been destroyed. The Welsh once lived there, but the ground has been torn asunder, and no fires are lit there now, nor are human voices to be heard calling to one another on the slopes. The poet refers to the flooding of the parish. The chapel has disappeared, no hymn rings out, and the last service has been held there. Today, the place belongs to the waters of the newly constructed lake, and the valley has lost its altar. The disturbing of graves for the building of the reservoir is a point of controversy, their peace has been violated, the cemetry mutilated, and the machines pulverises the landscape, uprooting rush and sedge.

Once the mountain-population had been evacuated, a process of afforestation began. Today, short miles from the coast, the landscape of north Ceredigion is characterised by large coniferous forests. As the trees matured in the 1970s and 80s, these plantations contributed to concealing traces of earlier inhabitation and culture, and access from valley to valley along old paths was reduced, thus making of the heaths and uplands a deserted place where less than a century before there had been intense activity.

The impact of the forests had not yet reached its full force during the decades when J.R. Jones was in his prime, but in his work we find ample reference to the plantations. A good example is to be found in the series *Ymson y Mynydd* (*The Mountain Speaks*), in a text entitled *Plannu Coed* (*Tree-Planting*). The piece begins with allusions to the small-holdings where the one-storey houses stand empty. The offspring of the last generation to drive the plough have abandoned the mountain to the curlew, and followed the road to a place from which they will never return.

The mountain then speaks of the forest-workers, of the contractors and their steel vehicles, of their meddling and relandscaping, men for whom the very name of the mountain is foreign and unpronounceable. The mountain denies the armies of trees in their efforts to efface evidence of its earlier history. Its scars remain, angry and purple, like weals on hands that have been ravaged by work.

Man's relationship with his environment is central to the poetry of J.R. Jones. A number of images re-occur in this context, with them a vocabulary that characterises the work. The words *tyddyn* and *tyddynwyr,* smallholding and smallholders, echo through the corpus. With them the tools used to work the land. The *aradr, plough,* a word used in the title of J.R. Jones first book, is emblematic. So to *oged, pladur* and *picwarch,* harrow, scythe and pitchfork respectively. We note here that, rather than considering the earth itself in any way amorphous, conceited or abstract, reference is constantly to *mynydd, bryn, cwm, ffridd,* and *anialwch,* for example, mountain, hill, valley, heath, wilderness, and moreover to onomastic elements that contribute strongly to the forming of a narrative that underpins the poet's work and vision. We find *Pont-y-Geifr, Tabor, Cwm Eleri, Moel Darren, Llangynfelyn, Craig y Felin* and *Cae Gwynt,* for example. Also, people here are named after their place of residence, and J.R. Jones refers to Ifan y Foel, Ifan of the Hill, for example. Here, the synonymity of man and place is part of the narrative that animates an environment.

Man, and his environment, animated through this shared narrative, is part in turn of a biotope that is home also to numerous species of flora and fauna, some wild some domestic, each enjoying its own right to occupy the environment in a way that contributes to an over-riding harmony or intrinsic balance, as perceived and described by the poet. The poetry is driven by a need to record this harmony and balance, and recreate it in verse, and this need is nourished, ironically, by invasion of the environment by intrusive or alien elements – landlord, tourist, machine, and, as we have seen above, the pine forests.

Movement from the environment through emigration is offset by movement towards the environment through immigration, all these combining to bring to the work of J.R. Jones its tension, pitch and poignancy. In this context, we cite three examples: *Atgofion* (*Memories*), *Ymwelwyr* (*Visitors*), and first *Y Golled* (*Loss*), taken from *Cerddi Cwm Eleri* (1980), J.R. Jones' third and final collection. This is the only poem in over thirty volumes of 20th century Ceredigion verse in which the task and ritual of sheep-shearing is described in detail. The world of man and flock on the mountain is depicted as having being harmonious before the trees were planted. Where once neighbours lived together, where once husbandry was practiced, where once a community thrived, now the soil has been conquered by the trees. The names of the old fields have disappeared, and through this loss the older narrative has been interrupted. In the forest, parcels of land are reduced to mere numbers. One section of the poem describes the sheep-shearing, when all give their best until finally the pens are emptied. The last fleece is bundled into the bulging sacks, and sheep and lambs dart through the mountain gate, free of their woollen coats.

Taken as a whole, the work of J.R. Jones sheds light on

three periods in the history of north Ceredigion, and Wales. In it we find a folk memory of the nineteenth century, a time of hardship and deprivation for the people, subjugated to the landlord, and compelled to labour in abysmal conditions in the local mines. Secondly, a time of happier years is depicted. The reader may begin to suspect a certain idealisation on the poet's part, but here we must distinguish between his medium – a form of verse between romanticism and modernism – and the actual historical facts. For the common people, the quality of life in west Wales improved significantly between the nineteenth and mid-twentieth century. However, this period, as others before it, soon elapses, and change heralds its arrival once again. In the third period, therefore, we find the world of the latter decades of the twentieth century, where mechanisation, tourism, mobility, migration, urbanisation, and afforestation are key-words.

The poem *Tan-y-Graig* in the collection *Rhwng Cyrn yr Aradr* (*Driving the Plough*) captures very much of the world J.R. Jones knew as a boy and a young man. It is a monument to that world, and to part of the history of Wales, its people and its language. The imagery is familiar in the context of the school of writing to which it belongs, the rural school of mid-twentieth century Ceredigion. In *Tan-y-Graig,* the weather erodes the lime plaster on the walls and spits hailstones through the perforated roof. The desolation is compounded by reference to the rust that has consumed the latch, and to the wire that now serves as a lock. The door squeaks in the clutches of the wind. With these words, we bid farewell to J.R. Jones and to the mountains of north Ceredigion.

FFYNNONLOYW
STORI
TAIR
CENHEDLAETH
GAN
MOELONA

A Universal View – Three Poems by Dic Jones, J.M. Edwards and Isgarn

Traditionally, the world of the rural bards is well defined. Their work in the 19th century reflects the passing of time, and chronicles events in their community. In the 20th century, this continues to be the case. Just as the medieval bard wrote elegies (*marwnad* or *galarnad*), eulogies (*moliant*), and satire (*dychan* or *gwawd*), so too does the rural bard in the 20th century, and just as the medieval bard sings the wedding (*neithior*) of a noble patron, his modern successor celebrates the marriage (*priodas*) of a friend or neighbour. There are however parallel developments, and occasionally poems occur where the expectations of the audience are not part of the poet's motivation for writing. In such a case, the work migrates temporarily and occupies another space.

In this chapter, as a precursor to a detailed examination of work by selected individuals, we look at three examples of compositions where the poet sees beyond the horizons of his immediate environment. These are *Y Fforest* (*The Forest*) by Dic Jones (*Agor Grwn,* p. 33); *Héloïse at Abélard* (*Héloïse writes to Abélard*), by J. M. Edwards (*Cerddi Ddoe a Heddiw,* p. 45), and *Dan y Coed* (*Under the Trees*), by Isgarn (*Caniadau Isgarn,* p. 45).

First we consider *From Héloïse to Abélard,* by J.M. Edwards. Born in 1903, J.M. Edwards moved to Barry in the mid-thirties. In his work, we find valuable descriptions of life in Ceredigion in the first quarter of the 20th century, as well as reflections on the world of the day. Here we introduce a unique poem, not only in Edwards' own work, but in the context of Welsh poetry as a whole. The poem is a letter from Héloïse to Abélard.

Pierre Abélard was born in Pallet, France in 1079. By

about 1110, he was a renowned theologian and an acclaimed teacher. His work however was the object of much criticism, and his ideas met with opposition. In 1115, he accepted a post tutoring a woman from an aristocratic family, some twenty years younger than him. He and his pupil Héloïse became lovers. In 1116, Héloïse gave birth to a son. After the birth, the pair married. The relationship and marriage were however not approved of by Héloïse's family, who took revenge on Abélard for having taken advantage of the young woman. On the order of her uncle, a man called Fulbert, and without any legal proceedings, Abélard was castrated. After this brutal attack, and the scandal that arose around it, Abélard withdrew to the monastery of St Denis, while Héloïse was sent to the convent at Argenteuil.

Lovers, parents of a son, man and wife, the pair were destined to live apart from then on, Héloïse a nun, later abbotess at Argenteuil, Abélard an influential and controversial philosopher, practicing at various locations in France. Pierre Abélard died in 1142. Héloïse was buried by his side in 1164. The story of Héloïse and Abélard is one of the great medieval romances of Europe, and its poignant tragedy became the subject of numerous texts. Interestingly, there seems to be no reference to it in Welsh tradition. In Britain, it is likely that the novel *Peter Abélard* by Helen Waddell (1933) brought the story to the attention of a literary public outside medievalist circles, and that J.M. Edwards became aware of it, either directly or indirectly, in this way.

J.M. Edward's letter from Héloïse to Abélard is inspired by the original 12th century correspondence between the two. Broken-hearted and distressed, destined never again to see the father of her child, Héloïse finally succumbs to the wish to write to Abélard from the convent. He replies, and so develops a series of letters, in Latin, that survived and were translated. The original letters are long. Héloïse's first contains about 4,000 words. Abélard's response is 3,000 words long. Héloïse continues with another 4,000-word epistle. Abélard's second reply runs to 8,000 words or so. The collection gives us detailed insight into their minds and hearts. While Abélard's writing remains didactic at many times, the tone of Héloïse's words is more tender and emotionally sincere. This is the tone adopted by J.M. Edwards in his composition.

He imagines the woman receiving a letter from her former lover, after dark and unrelenting years. The letter is a balm to her, and, reading its tender words, her own name entwined in its lines, health is restored to her soul, provisionally at least. Happy to have received the letter, it nonetheless unleashes on her a flood of memories regarding the past misfortunes of the pair. However, both peace and life are reignited in her heart as she learns that Abélard's love remains steadfast as the deep rock beneath the convent where she lives. This love, and memory of it, is the fortress in which she finds her defence.

J.M. Edwards' letter from Héloïse to Abélard continues to describe how the memory of separation from her lover after their passionate embraces is as a wound to one who is already weak. However, despite the storm of emotion unleashed, receiving the letter, she says, is sufficient comfort for her. The poet displays remarkable sensibility as he writes the closing lines of the letter. Héloïse beseeches Abélard not to forget her entirely, and asks that he send comfort to her soon in the form of another letter. She asks whether Abélard can see the ocean from where he now lives, adding in conclusion that tide and ocean once accompanied the fervent duo formed by the harmony of their two hearts. This refined and sophisticated piece of writing by J.M. Edwards has no equivalent amongst the work of his peers and fellows, and is worlds apart from the homely rhymes of the 19th century *bardd gwlad* or folk poet.

Next we consider *The Forest* by Dic Jones. The poem is located in the Alps. It is an allegory that tells of a shepherd who plants oak trees to provide shelter from the biting mountain wind. Ultimately, his work helps turn the wilderness into cultivated land. The poem is narrated in the third person, and from the point of view of a traveller who visits and revisits the great mountain chain twice in the course of his life and in the course of the poem. During his first visit, he roams as he pleases along the rocky Alpine slopes that had never known the point of the harrow. Then the narrator meets a shepherd who is sorting a heap of acorns in his bucket. The traveller resumes his journey, leaving the shepherd to plant acorns in the moss. Many years later, the traveller returns to find a forest. Swaying on the steep incline of the hill, he sees rows of tall oak trees, a forest where once nothing grew. This is a unique poem in the work of Dic Jones. Written early in his career, it is an example of venturing beyond the limits of his immediate environment, a thing the poet does not repeat in this way in his later career. Unlike the traveller, the poet does not return to a place beyond the horizon to find there new wonder and fulfilment.

The third poem we look at it this chapter is *Dan y Coed* (Under the Trees) by Isgarn. A word of introduction is required. In the body of poetry that we have inherited in Ceredigion, a sense of camaraderie is often pronounced, a sense of community strong. This is reflected in the primary work of the poets, in the anecdotes surrounding their meetings, and in some of the photographic evidence that accompanies the written material. The mood is jovial and humorous in the poetic dialogue of the community, especially in the south of the county. Importantly, if images of the rural poet – *y bardd gwlad* – as a buoyant character, at ease in his community, and sure of his values – religious, linguistic and cultural – are ones we come across in Ceredigion in the 20th century, then these images are balanced by the realisation through reading the work of Isgarn, for example, that man may feel alienated from his fellows even when firmly rooted in a given territory.

Isgarn remained alone all his life in the hills beyond Tregaron where he tended his flocks, and in the poem *Dan y Coed* (*Under the Trees*) he stands typically at a distance from society, contemplating a funeral scene. The funeral is modest, the mourners poor and simple, and only some of the fellow parishioners of the deceased come to accompany the aged pilgrim on his final journey through the world. Despite their loss, they shoulder their burden willingly. The poem then transcends the scene, and Isgarn writes the following remarkable line: 'The river wept because its foaming sourcelet was so distant from the wave'.

Rather than simply depicting what he sees with lyrical skill and with sympathy for his fellows, the poet finds a poetic *idea,* and succeeds in expressing it vividly and succinctly. As the funeral passes, the river weeps too, not however out of pity for the mortal, dead or living, but because of the nature of its own being. This line seems to redefine the relationship between man and nature that prevails in modern times, a relationship in which man and nature are distinct from one another, this perception both reflecting and contributing to man's alienation from the world. Isgarn, in this line, while observing the funeral, makes the world whole again, thus alleviating the burden of death, but without seeking to defy death in any way.

The poem ends with a verse that includes the phrase 'the dead of this world'. These, the living dead, step lightly homeward after the funeral, while one of the small community, their brother whom they have buried, remains in the cemetery to live beneath the trees. Isgarn is expressing a non-fragmented view of the world. The river flows and weeps, from source to sea. Man in his existence is part-life, part-death at all times. Time moves forward, but there seems to be no rupture between present and future.

Yr Aradr
Gymreig
FFRANSIS PAYNE
E.M.R

Dic Jones – The Final Flourish of the Tradition

'Those who tend the earth,' writes Dic Jones in a poem called Daear (*Earth*) in the collection *Sgubo'r Storws* (*Sweeping the Storehouse*), 'ensure the world shall spin and shall not stop'. A farmer from near Aberporth, his work is the culmination of a hundred years of lyric endeavour in South Ceredigion, and of centuries of classical tradition in rural West Wales. His twin odes, *Gwanwyn* (*Spring*) and *Cynhaeaf* (*Harvest*) are the ultimate expression in modern times of man's ancient covenant with the earth, a covenant broken in the industrial age, and all but forgotten in the technological era.

Born in Pen-y-Graig in the parish of Llancynfelyn in Northern Ceredigion near the Dyfi estuary and overlooking the peatland of Cors Fochno, the poet-to-be moved to Southern Ceredigion at an early age for family reasons. There he spent his life, attending school in nearby Cardigan town, later electing to dedicate himself to ploughing the acres of Hendre Farm. His publishing career began early, and in 1960, aged 27, his first collection appeared. The title, *Agor Grwn* (*Opening a Furrow*), captures two things: the subject-matter that defines the poet's world, and a presage of the depth and breadth of the field from which the poet would draw inspiration during his career.

Dic Jones stands on the edge of two worlds. One, the traditional agrarian society that lingered in Ceredigion until the Second World War, is a world he experienced as a child. The other, a mechanised world where horizons widen and man's experience of his environment tends to be incomplete and fragmented, is the world in which he lived his adult life. The former is a world of humble cottages, the latter of two-storey slate-roofed houses, the former of the modest small-holding or *tyddyn*, the latter the world of the industrial farm.

One was the world of the horse, the other of the tractor, one of candlelight the other of electricity. The former was the world of the landlord, the latter a world in which the farmer enjoyed the right to propriety of his own land. In the world of the cottage, horse and candlelight, the bard in West Wales composed *tribannau, rhigymau* – forms of light verse – and some ballads. Much of the work was anonymous, just as the tenants on the large estates were anonymous. In the decades after 1900, the tenor of the writing changes, as the people and their poets assume a new air of confidence. Dic Jones was born into this time.

The confidence that characterises the world in which Dic Jones grew up is essential to the flourishing of his work. *Gwanwyn* (*Spring*) and *Cynhaeaf* (*Harvest*) celebrate the perennial bounty of the soil, and the renewal of the bounty, a cycle that brings order into the world and allows man to know and to enjoy the meaning of fulfilment. In writing these two odes, Dic Jones was writing within a tradition, and other poets in Ceredigion had written of the harvest before he did so. One such was the shepherd Isgarn who speaks of the torn hands who planted hope, turning the earth into a sea of golden acres, like molten metal in the flowing wind. In 1925, Isfoel also sang of the harvest. His poem is retrospective, and paints a picture of harvest-tide in the pre-mechanised era. He tells how the traditional harvesters have disappeared, how the heroes wielding their sickles are no more, and how the voice of the foreman shouting the order for the blades to be sharpened no longer rings out over the field.

In *The Agricultural Community in South-West Wales at the Turn of the Twentieth Century* (pp 3-4) on the other hand, David Jenkins confirms the resilience of traditional techniques in Ceredigion. 'During the summer of 1959,' he writes, 'I watched men cutting corn with a scythe and binding it by hand in a North Cardiganshire valley within twelve miles of Aberystywth. As late as 1951, the reaping hook was used in mid Cardiganshire to save the crop during a difficult harvest'.

Alun Cilie writes a long account of the harvest in his *Y Cynhaeaf* (*The Harvest*). Youngest of the Cilie clan, Alun was born at the turn of the century, and remembers the scenes of communal labour that he witnessed as a boy. The poem is probably inspired by change and mechanisation, though this is not stated in the text as such. Dic Jones' *Harvest,* on the other hand, is set in the mechanised age, and the poem balances between the two worlds, evoking sentiment that avoids degenerating into nostalgia, while uniting old and new in a vision that identifies agriculture in both ages as manifestations of the same bond with the earth. In the closing lines of *Harvest,* Dic Jones pens a statement that expresses his vision of the role of the farmer in the world. As long as man walks the earth, he says, husbandry and farming will continue to be practiced, and the tradition will be passed on from one generation to the next. Elaborating on this idea, he writes that while winter still comes and goes, so too will the harvest be gathered in. Man will continue to work the soil, and the world shall be blessed with fertility while the sun continues to shine.

The long strict-metre poem *Gwanwyn* (*Spring*) is a sister-text to *Cynhaeaf* (*Harvest*). The two *awdl* – odes – share the same elevated and incantatory idiom, the same sweep and majesty. In *Gwanwyn* (*Spring*), the poet suggests that despite the tribulations that it is man's lot to endure, the plough gives human endeavour much meaning, and brings with it contentment on the one hand, and the promise of future fulfilment on the other. While birds still mate in the wood, the spring shall impart its treasures for all time to come. While cattle continue to graze, man shall harvest the fruit of the earth, and his offspring shall reseed their plots. *Gwanwyn* (*Spring*) moves through passages descriptive, reflective, and philosophic. For the farmer, writes Dic Jones, the moorland holds an elusive charm that is older than yearning, the foal and the lamb host a timeless youth that is continuously renewed, and each shoot contains the ancestry of its species.

The idea of two parallel worlds has been introduced above, the world of landlord and tenant, and the world of increased confidence amongst the people in West Wales. This period of confidence is however short-lived in its simplicity. The destruction wrought by two world wars ushers in a new duality in people's minds. On the one hand, ironically, the older world of tenant and landlord grows to symbolise a certain stability. On the other, the world in the mid-twentieth century becomes synonymous with destruction. As a result of this destruction, man grasps for truths that he hopes may guide him, but finds only confusion, scepticism and doubt. In Welsh culture, these doubts cast their shadow on religious life. In turn, as times change, the future of the Welsh language itself is surrounded by doubt. In the work of Dic Jones, in a culture where conviction and endurance were virtues, these doubts find their way into print, but only on a handful of occasions. The first example occurs early in the poet's career in the form of a poem entitled *Cyffes* (*Confession*) in the collection *Caneuon Cynhaeaf* (*Harvest Songs*). The poem sounds a dissonant note in the social and aesthetic harmony that is the rock on which the collection is built, and is the earliest evidence in the poet's work of psychological distress. Dic Jones contends that reason has blinded him, preventing him from seeing things that are clear. Moreover, contemporary ideas regarding knowledge have simply prevented him from believing things that are true. He compares himself to a fairgoer who loses his senses in the bustle and excitement of the fair-ground. Distinctions between virtue and vice are blurred, heaven and hell are mere words.

Prey to these doubts, as others of his generation, the poet briefly revisits the matter in a memorable sonnet, *Mewn Llythyr* (*In a Letter*). Significantly, this is the opening poem in the collection *Sgubo'r Storws* (*Sweeping the Storehouse*), thus setting the tone of the collection from the outset. The poem describes the waning of youthful energy and fervour, and how, with the passing of the years, neither joy nor grief retain their earlier poignancy. Appearing through a gap in the clouds at night, the moon seems brighter than the dawn. A brief moment of calm during a storm may seem overbearingly loud. The salmon pursues its journey back to the spawning beds, leaping all the higher to clear the rapids when the pool beneath is deepest. However, man's lot, it seems to Dic Jones in this sonnet, is to feel the passion of his early years replaced by an all-consuming grey.

In the work of Dic Jones, and others in Ceredigion in the 20th century, both the traditional and modern worlds inform the writing in various ways. The former tends to represent a certain harmony, between man and nature for example. This harmony finds a ready vehicle in the classical Welsh metres practiced by Dic Jones and others in the bardic milieu of which he was a member. Just as the twin pillars of a Greek temple rise unadorned, smooth and symmetrical to support the weight of the sober edifice, classical Welsh metre, whether medieval or post-medieval, is a statement of order, balance and stability in the world. The 20th century, however, is not a time of order, balance and stability. It is a time of destruction and disharmony, of imbalance and of fragmentation, all this leading to the inner doubts, fears and despair that characterise the period. The pre-modern period, it may be said, was marked by the struggle between dogma and perceived heresies. Scientific discovery and rationalism succeeds this order of things. Enlightenment and rationalism is in turn overtaken by totalitarian creeds, and by the hegemony of the machine. This is the period during which Dic Jones' career unfolded. However, the clash between classical, pre-modern harmony and the shadows cast by the concerns of the modern day rest largely unresolved in his work.

Two poems from *Sgubo'r Storws* (*Sweeping the Storehouse*) serve to illustrate this. *Sweeping the Storehouse* is Dic Jones' fourth collection. It was published thirty-six years after his collection *Agor Grwn* (*Opening a Furrow*) appeared, the four volumes published during this period being the equivalent of a volume per decade or so. *Sweeping the Storehouse* is a revealing title. Through it, the poet suggests that he is nearing the end of an era. By now, 1986, the fraternity and *hwyl* of the Cilie circle has vanished. Dic Jones is bereft of his local bardic companions.

For many years, the Aberporth farmer wore the mantle of the quick-tongued *extempore* composer of sophisticated, light-hearted verse. He was a popular public figure who entertained audiences and conformed to the archetype of the rural bard. He was the voice of his people. By 1986 however, according to evidence from certain poems, the poet suffered inwardly, at least on occasion, from feelings of uncertainty. The poem *Wynebau* (*Faces*) is one of two insights into an inner world that he was thereafter to keep locked away from his readers and audiences. He speaks of the other side that he perceives to the face he calls his own, a side that is, he believes, hidden even to those dearest to him. This hidden face stares back at him from the mirror.

The poem *Miserere,* also from the collection *Sweeping the Storehouse,* underlines the cold *angst* expressed in *Wynebau* (*Faces*). The text is a cri *de coeur* in which the poet admits that others may suffer greater tribulation than he, but contends that the suffering of others brings no relief to an afflicted heart. Night and its towering ghosts threaten to engulf the poet in *Miserere,* and dawn's glimmer seems distant and remote. In this poem, we find a man battling with depression, and possibly ill-equipped to deal with it. In *Wynebau* (*Faces*), Dic Jones briefly admits to a darkness that inhabits him, but immediately announces there are things to which he will not confess. In these lines, the poet closes the door on his other face, leaving unexplored the unlit cellars and lofts of the mind and heart in which modernism finds a large part of its riches.

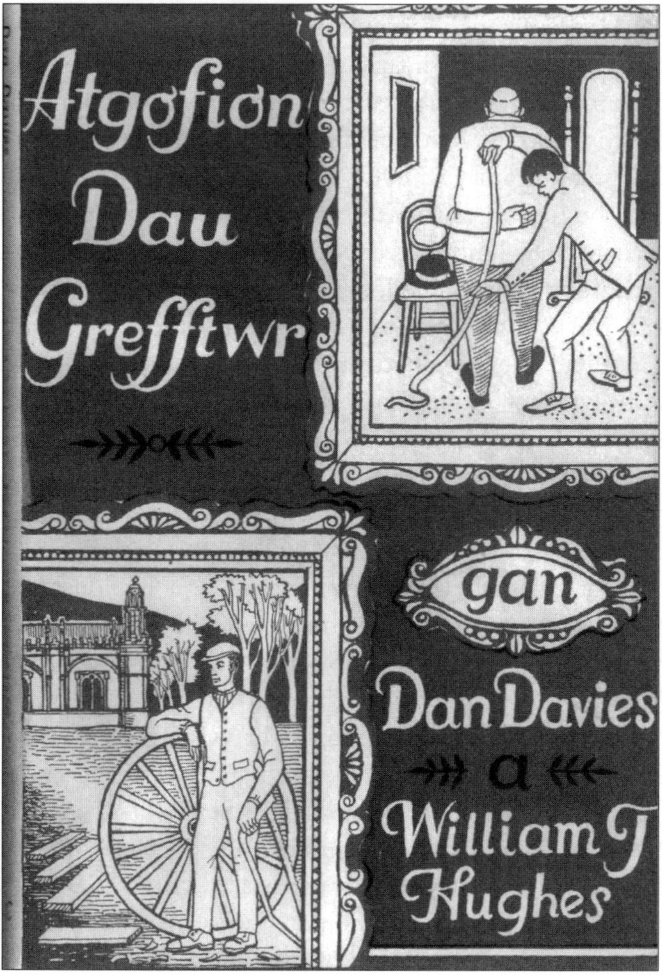
Atgofion
Dau
Grefftwr
gan
Dan Davies
a
William J
Hughes

The Influence of the Cilie Family on Dic Jones

In his autobiography, *Os hoffech wybod,* p. 131, Dic Jones speaks of his earliest brushes with poetry and how his career began to take shape. We quote the following remarks from the book: 'Though I can't be sure why it all [i.e. writing poetry] sprouted in the first place, I am perfectly sure of one reason for its growing later'. This reason was 'support from the community'. The Jones brothers of Cilie Farm, between Llangrannog and Cwmtydu, better known as *bois y Cilie,* the Cilie boys, were part of this community, and they were to influence Dic Jones' career both directly and profoundly. In his autobiography, Dic Jones writes (*Os hoffech Wybod,* pp 132-133): 'Unknown to me, my father had met Alun Cilie...and mentioned to him...that 'the younger son is showing some interest in verse'. 'Really!' came the answer, 'send him over and we'll see what he's made of'. And so 'see what he was made of' was the order of things for the next two winters or so, and on Sunday nights I would visit the Cilie farm'.

Out of these winter evenings grew a life-long bond between master and pupil. In several poems, Dic Jones refers to Alun Cilie, his mentor. In *Englynion Coffa Alun Cilie* (*Verses in Memory of Alun Cilie*) in the collection *Storom Awst* (*August Storm*) for example, he writes that St David's Day marks the passing of a beloved member of a legendary family. Alun Cilie, we note, died on St David's Day 1975. Now that his teacher has fallen silent, Dic Jones longs for the Cilie of old, and he speaks of his desire to drink long of the sweet mead of the deceased master's irretrievable craft.

A sonnet in memory of Alun Cilie from *Storom Awst* (*August Storm*) entitled *Yn Angladd Alun* (*At Alun's Funeral*) tells us more about Dic Jones' teacher. The bard describes him as an old craftsman, someone for whom there is no longer room in the literature of the modern age. Dic Jones reminds us in his sonnet that Alun Cilie belonged to the older bardic tradition where orality was a driving force. The old master, we are told, reproduced everything from the reservoir of the mind, whether classical *cynghanedd* or sonnets and lyrics. Now, he concludes, his idiom has been committed to the earth.

Dic Jones also had deep respect for Dafydd Jones (Isfoel), an older brother of Alun's, and in *Storom Awst,* we find a poem dedicated to *Isfoel.* He compares Isfoel to the druids of the ancient world who climbed to the hilltops to face the light, holding the moon in their hand. Dic Jones' respect for Isfoel's wit and eloquence was shared by the bardic community of West Wales in the early and mid-20th century.

While the environment into which Dic Jones was born was thoroughly Welsh, the poet became aware of the wider world at an early age. 'In the final years of the war,' he writes (*Os Hoffech Wybod,* p. 140), 'a number of foreigners from various European countries lived in our midst, Italians and Germans, prisoners of war who had been brought to the camp in Henllan, Poles who had been expelled from their motherland...We were therefore quite a cosmopolitan society, and as a result were perfectly well placed to compare the attitudes of different peoples to living in a foreign country'. In his youth, the poet became close to members of other national groups: 'How many times I shared a fine meal with them [i.e. the prisoners of war who helped with the farm-work] at the bottom of the valley here, a rabbit roasted on two bricks on an open fire, or a trout from the stream'. (*Os Hoffech Wybod,* p. 141).

These experiences inform a view of humanity as expressed in *I'm Cydnabod* (*To the People I Know*), the first poem in his first collection *Agor Grwn* (*Opening a Furrow*).

In the poem, he expresses the idea that, throughout history, all past human experience of the world is perpetuated in the behaviour and culture of the living. No smile ever smiled, no scowl ever scowled has been lost since the first dawn, and all craft passed on from hand to hand still forms part of someone somewhere in the world. The poet considers himself indebted to all mankind, and thanks every person whose path he crosses, no matter what their racial background may be. They are all, he says, part of the cloth from which he himself was made.

Dic Jones became synonymous in his earlier years with *Cynhaeaf* (*Harvest*), in mid-career with *Gwanwyn* (*Spring*), and in later years with the many poems he wrote for members of his community as befitted a Welsh bard. Close examination of *Agor Grwn* and *Cynhaeaf* however reveals other work overshadowed either by poems acclaimed or popular. One such is *Y Fforest,* a text analysed in the chapter *Beyond The Horizons*. Another poem is *Gŵr ysydd ar Drwm Grwsâd* (*A Man Pursuing an Arduous Crusade*) from the collection *Caneuon Cynhaeaf* (*Harvest Songs*). Unlike other work by Dic Jones and his fellow bards, this poem does not attempt to appeal to the sentiments. It does not rely on imagery or figurative speech, and is not concerned with the aesthetic pleasures of verse. It deals in abstract ideas, and is set out with didactic rigour.

The poem is a dialogue between two aspects of the poet's reaction to a man who undertakes to convince others of the validity of an argument that is difficult to defend. Most unusually, we are not told who the man is and what the argument may be. The tension in the poem is between, on the one hand, the admiration the poet feels for his subject, and a feeling of inadequacy that stems from knowing that he the poet does not have the courage to challenge the majority, as does his subject. The poem is classical in more than once sense, not only linguistically, with its use of strict metre, but also intellectually, expounding as it does parallel arguments, thesis and antithesis.

In one verse the poet states that this man, pursuing his difficult crusade, arouses in him inexplicable affection, and that it is often the weaker party in a battle who is most likely to win our sympathies. Seeing him, the poet enjoys the feeling of standing on safe ground. Hearing the very sound of this man's voice, the poet feels himself convinced, but feels himself lowly and serf-like, lacking the courage to act according to his passions. There is no evidence in Dic Jones' work after 1969 of thinking in this abstract vein. It seems likely that the *genre* found limited appeal amongst his peers.

After *Agor Grwn* (1960), *Caneuon Cynhaeaf* (1969). *Storom Awst* (1978) and *Sgubo'r Storws* (1986), Dic Jones published three further collections of verse. Two are a collection of verse written on a weekly basis for a Welsh-language magazine, *Golwg,* in which the poet visits subjects from the newsroom. The third *Cerddi Gwlad Dic Jones* (*The Folk Poems of Dic Jones*), published posthumously in 2012, is largely a collection of pieces written for individuals from his community to celebrate or mark different occasions. His career falls into three periods. The first begins with his introduction to his mentor, fellow farmer Alun Cilie, and ends with Alun Cilie's death in 1975. The second period is brief, lasting from the time of Alun Cilie's death until the publishing of *Sgubo'r Storws* in 1986 after which a longer period begins, one that lasts until the poet's death in 2009. During this quarter of a century, Dic Jones remained an establishment figure, writing each week in *Golwg* and attending the *Eisteddfod,* before being appointed Arch-Druid shortly before his death.

DAVID JENKINS
The Agricultural
Community in
South-West Wales
at the turn of the
Twentieth Century

Isgarn – The Outsider

In the rural poetry of 20th century Ceredigion, a sense of camaraderie among the bards and poets is often pronounced, and a sense of solidarity and fraternity is strong. The mood is often jovial in the poetic dialogue of the fraternity, especially in the south of the county. We might cite Alun Cilie's *Y Pwdl*, an elegy in *cywydd*-form to a poodle, a theme visited too by Dic Jones in his *Marwnad y Pwdl*, (*Elegy for a Poodle*). Isfoel in his turn also takes up this unconventional theme in the collection *Ail Gerddi Isfoel*, his second collection.

Composing humorous verse of this type was a pastime for the wordsmith, an opportunity for him to keep his tools sharpened. During the twentieth century, thousands of *englynion* – rhyming quatrains – were composed, many on the perennial Welsh theme of gravestone epitaphs. One tells how an insurance broker has taken his chatter to the tomb. Another, somewhat laconically, describes having a tooth pulled. There are *englynion* to the mini-skirt, the electric light-bulb, a Russian rocket, a local tenor who is somewhat overweight, and countless other topics of conversation and discussion, all delivered with sparkling wit and bardic skill.

Not all the poets of the time shared equally in the warmth of the bardic brotherhood however. One such outsider was Isgarn (Richard Davies). Born in 1887 in Trawscoed, in the hills of central Ceredigion, Isgarn died in 1947, and bequeathed his work and some money to the National Library of Wales, requesting that they use the gift to publish a volume of his work posthumously. *Caniadau Isgarn* (*The Poems of Isgarn*), a slim volume containing 52 pages of poetry, appeared in Aberystwyth in 1949, printed by the National Library of Wales, and edited by T.H. Parry Williams.

In the book's opening text, *Y Gors* (*The Bog*), the reader is invited to visit Cors Caron Bog near Tregaron, a desolate tract of unfarmed land where neither village nor homestead may be found. This text sets the tone for much of the content of the book.

Shepherd and bachelor, Isgarn lived a secluded life. On occasion, he comments on his lot, revealing part of his inner world in a modern way atypical of the rural poetry of the time. In *A Welais yn y Rhyl* (*Things I saw in Rhyl*), he sees two of various things, including two nuns, and two people on a tandem bicycle, and asks whether it is a rule of life that these things exist in pairs while he walks alone, failing to conform to the rule. This feeling of isolation from human society recurs in the volume. On his way to hospital in Aberystwyth some months before his death, the poet writes in *Ffarwél* (*Farewell*) that he is similar to the old black sheep that, just as he does, carries in her fleece the mark of an untamed hybrid.

While Isgarn remained a bachelor throughout his life, in *Caniadau Isgarn*, he writes twice in direct terms of women he met or knew. In *Pentir Llŷn* (*The Llŷn Peninsula*), the mood is romantic but cautious. If you ever go to the Llŷn Peninsula, he advises the reader, do not reveal any of your secrets to the girl I met there. The second direct allusion to a woman he knew occurs in the *englyn* entitled *Hen Ferch* (*An Old Girl*). The woman, he claims, tried to encourage him with a wink and a nod, but the bard keeps well away from her little cottage, ultimately calling her an old scarecrow, in keeping with the conventions of rhyme and ridicule in the *englyn* tradition.

The poem *Cân y Cowman* (*Song of the Cowman*) brings us into another corner of the rural space, one where Isgarn depicts another fellow solitary male figure. He empathises with the cowman, a brother in mountain farming, whose song brightens up the yard despite his being exposed to the elements before daybreak and after nightfall. The poem ends however on a note of solitude, tinged perhaps with longing, though without hearing the poet read his text we cannot know what the intonation of the closing lines might have been. Now Isgarn writes that after his season's work, the cowman too will enjoy a lady's company at the bustling winter fair in a nearby seaside town – Aberystwyth, in all probability.

There is humour in the *englynion* of Isgarn too, in *Tegell* (*A Kettle*), and *Y Gamblwr* (*The Gambler*), for example. However, he reveals himself in his work to be prey to the doubts and shadows that may inhabit any human mind whether in an urban or in a rural space. The theme of mortality recurs in *Deilen Grin* (*A Withered Leaf*), *Y Gwely* (*The Bed*), *Ar Ddiwedd F'Oes* (*At The End of My Days*) and *Dan y Coed* (*Beneath the Trees*), for example, and of man's short life-span in *Yr Ywen* (*The Yew Tree*), *Y Fawnen* (*Peatland*), and *Y Trothwy* (*The Threshold*) to name three other *englynion*.

Importantly then, if images of the rural poet – *y bardd gwlad* – as a buoyant character, at ease in his community, and sure of his values – religious, linguistic and cultural – are ones we come across in Ceredigion in the 20th century, these images are balanced by the realisation through reading the work of Isgarn that a man may feel alienated from his fellows even when firmly rooted in a given territory. As well as a feeling of alienation, a sense of conflict between man and the universe occurs on occasion in the work of Isgarn. This conflict is one side of a relationship with the world whose other side is sometimes expressed in terms of harmony, union and elation. These two reciprocal things occur in the poems *Nesu Adref* (*Approaching Home*), *Y Nos* (*Night*), two very similar texts, and thirdly in *Y Porth Prydferth* (*The Splendid Gateway*).

In *Y Porth Prydferth*, a sonnet inspired by a rainbow, the poet continues to demonstrate how natural phenomena inform his view of the world. More precisely, the poem demonstrates how apparent contradictions in the natural world and the resolution of these contradictions contribute to informing this view. He writes of the rainbow, saying that the eye has never witnessed its like, and that no human hand has ever wrought anything comparable. In this verse, Isgarn – unconsciously – echoes a line that recurs in early Welsh poetry. When an anonymous voice in the late first millennium AD sang '*Namyn Duw nid oes dewin*', 'Other than God, none can accomplish wonders', they were expressing a view similar to that expressed by Isgarn.

As the poem continues, the shepherd describes himself as a speechless worshipper, contemplating the rainbow as a master craftsman would contemplate a swirling pattern. Here, following directly the reference to the human eye and hand in lines three and four, the word '*addolwr*' 'worshipper' is carefully chosen, suggesting that the poet regards the beauty of the rainbow as a manifestation of divinity. This divinity is, however, in no way an overwhelming force. As the text continues, the poet does not tremble in awe, but looks skyward again and again, eyes full of wonder, discerning seven layers of strident colour. These colours soon expire, and now all that remains to be seen is a plain and unadorned sky. 'Where is the painter?' asks Isgarn, wondering whether the painter might be disillusioned, now that the sun is shining after the shower, and the rainbow's colours have disappeared.

This idea, that the creator of the rainbow may suffer disillusionment if the sun erases his or her work, does not concur with perceptions of God in the Abrahamic world, Christian, Muslim and Judaic, as an unquestionable wielder of absolute power. The idea is closer to traditions whose universe is governed by a pantheon of non-omnipotent gods. In such traditions, Celtic for example, the non-omnipotence of members of the pantheon is illustrated on occasion by ridicule or loss of face. Thus in *The Battle of Moytura* in Gaelic tradition, for example, the Dagda, god supreme of the Tuatha Dé Danann, is made to eat porridge by his captors the Fomorians, until his belly threatens to burst.

This reading of the text *Y Porth Prydferth* (*The Splendid Gateway*) enables us to further our understanding of man's relationship with the universe in the poetry of Isgarn. Although the number of poems we have to hand is modest, there is sufficient evidence for us to discern a pattern in the poet's ideas. Two other poems, similar in tone, where light and dark play major roles, are *Nesu Adref* (*Approaching Home*) and *Y Nos* (*The Night*). In both cases, night is perceived as being hostile to man. In *Nesu Adref* (*Approaching Home*), Isgarn describes walking home over moor and mountain, and how, in a state of exhaustion, he feels himself close to drawing his last breath. His heart almost dies within him, he says, and the night is bereft of hope. His faith is shaken and his mind remains troubled. This is the price he pays for having survived his nocturnal ordeal.

The poem *Y Nos* (*The Night*) tells how the daylight hours retreat as dark approaches, slowly charging the leaden sky with its mute paralysis. The night ripens, bringing with it silence to replace bright laughter, and stealing from view the gleaming lakes and tranquil pastures that are apparent while the sun is high. The poet rebels against the dying of the day, but his faith is restored on seeing a star shine tall upon night's peak. 'Foolish bard', he says, 'I could not but forget my anger'.

In both texts, night brings with it a sense of loss, or the

fear of imminent loss, but this is dispersed by various and unexpected manifestations of light that restore the poet's faith in the world. In *Nesu Adref* (*Approaching Home*), he writes of arriving home just before dawn, perhaps after a local *Eisteddfod,* perhaps during the lambing season, perhaps for another reason. Despite its enormity, the nearby mountain is indiscernible in the lingering dark. Then Isgarn sees a glimmer of dawn. The glimmer grows brighter, shedding its light like a lamp, and turning the black mountain into a mountain of white.

These three poems, *Y Porth Prydferth* (*The Splendid Gateway*), *Nesu Adref* (*Approaching Home*), and *Y Nos* (*The Night*), perpetuate an early view of the world held by man as a place oscillating between light and dark, night and day, winter and summer, hope and fear, faith and despair. This view of the world is an elemental one and stems from an intimate knowledge of nature and of the forces latent in nature. During a life spent on the mountain, Isgarn, so his poetry suggests, came to know and appreciate these forces in a way man had done for millennia before him.

In the englyn entitled *Ar Ddiwedd F'Oes* (*At the End of My Days*), Isgarn describes himself as an aged shepherd, raised in the deep tranquillity of the old Welsh mountains. He bids farewell, goes to die alone in hospital twenty miles away in Aberystwyth, and bequeaths some money to the National Library in the hope that they may publish some of his work after his death. I have seen no accounts in print of his funeral, and have heard none in local tradition. His contemporary Isfoel remembers him in three quatrains published in *Cerddi Isfoel,* and describes him as a modest man of few words who carried the torch of his calling and of his people.

Alone the shepherd and bard lived, and alone he remained until, somewhat ironically, in Aberystwyth hospital, only months from death, he spends a late hour in the company of his nurse. This is a rare if not unique instance of Isgarn's describing human interaction of which he himself is part. The poem is a sonnet entitled *Golygfa Ganol Nos* (*O Ysbyty Aberystwyth, 1946*), *Midnight Scene* (*From Aberystwyth Hospital, 1946*). In the ward, the patients all are sleeping peacefully. The moon is on its way across the hills of Llanbadarn Fawr parish, while the dead sleep in their graves beyond Pen Glais hill. And in the calm beyond the disturbed dream of the departed, nurse and bardic shepherd sit together, sharing a meal of four eggs.

Were it not for a copy of *Caniadau Isgarn* that my grandmother gave me in the 1980s, it is unlikely I would ever have heard of Isgarn. And were it not for her gift, these pages would not have been written in recognition of the genius of a solitary shepherd from the mountains of Ceredigion.

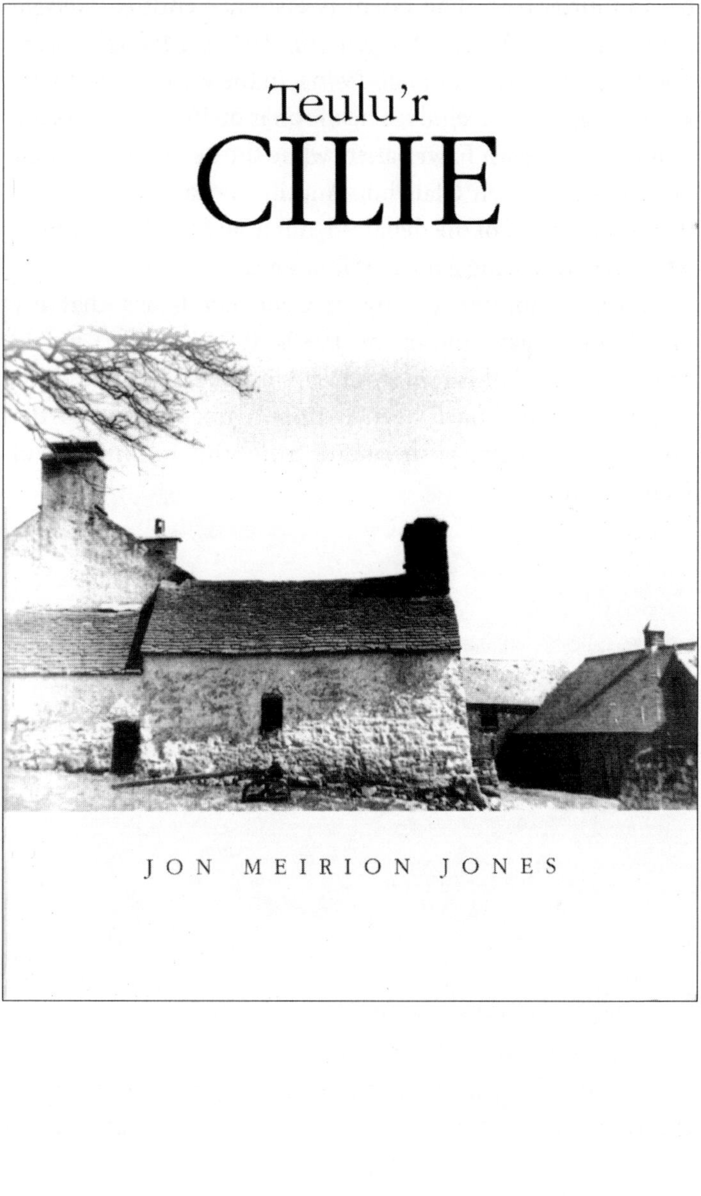
Teulu'r
CILIE
JON MEIRION JONES

B.T. Hopkins and J.M. Edwards: A View of the Cosmos

In the work of the Ceredigion poets, there are hundreds of compositions written to mark a social occasion, birth, death, marriage, and other passages from one stage of life to another. Of the remaining texts, about a quarter relate directly to the themes of the present study, *Pen and Plough*, and to man's relationship with the earth. A handful of other poems stand apart. Amongst these are two long texts in which we find expression of a distinctive view of the cosmos. This view is elaborated in the form of a long treatise, philosophical in tenor, by B.T. Hopkins. His *Bywyd a Byw* (*Life and Living*) (*Rhos Helyg a Cherddi Eraill*, pp 41-46), 148 lines long, has received little attention in Wales. This is true also of a similar text by J.M. Edwards, a poetic study in six movements entitled *Bywyd* (*Life*) (*Cerddi Ddoe a Heddiw* pp 13-15). The idea in these poems is that the world is a manifestation of an innate energy that flows through all things and thus unifies them.

In B.T. Hopkins' *Bywyd a Byw* (*Life and Living*), the emphasis is on unity, and culminates as follows 'Though I be a mere grain,' he writes, 'I am part of you, I place my trust in the great Entirety that is incomplete without the pieces I contribute, though my existence be brief and fleeting.'

In *Bywyd* (*Life*) from the collection *Cerddi Ddoe a Heddiw* by J.M. Edwards, the emphasis is on the unifying energy and the resultant motion that it causes in the world. 'I know that I and this integral whole are one being,' he writes, and 'part of the unfailing motion of all living things.' Ultimately however, this energy overwhelms J.M. Edwards, throwing his mind into turmoil, as we shall see below. On the other hand, B.T. Hopkins' *Bywyd a Byw* (*Life and Living*) is a sustained celebration of the energy that flows through the world, an energy that causes not turmoil, but elation.

Who was B.T. Hopkins, a modest Welsh hill-farmer, and how did he come to express this ancient view of the cosmos in a remote part of Ceredigion in the mid-twentieth century?

Ben T. Hopkins was born in 1897 in Lledrod, central Ceredigion, and is associated with nearby Mynydd Bach, an upland area of open commonage and windswept farmland. A selection of his work is extant in a 46-page long book published in 1976 by Cyhoeddiadau Modern Cymreig entitled *Rhos Helyg a Cherddi Eraill* (*Rhos Helyg and Other Poems*). The title takes its name from a poem, highly regarded locally and nationally in its day, in which the poet describes an abandoned homestead called Rhos Helyg.

Hopkins was almost eighty years old when this slim volume, his only book, was published, and the fact that the poems appeared in book-form at all is remarkable. The bardic milieu in Ceredigion was in large part dominated by an oral tradition, intended and designed to enrich community life and confirm certain values. Reading their publications closely however, we find rare jewels such *Bywyd a Byw* (*Life and Living*). The poem is a *tour-de-force* on the joys and tribulations of man's time on earth, two of whose recurring themes are the natural forces that animate the world, and the perennial renewal of the soil and the seasons. Hopkins writes of the ageless earth that has groaned since time began through wintry storms and hellfire heat, speaking of the pain and pangs endured so that the bright lily might bloom on the bare rocks.

In another verse the poet reiterates the mortal nature of the flesh, comparing it to straw that is soon dry and lifeless, only to find a comparison, the planet and a single grain, that serves to illustrate his thinking. Though his flesh be nothing more than a fistful of straw that will soon disappear, the poet climbs high above the earth to contemplate the dawn, just as like the tiny lark does. And the laws that govern the whole planet are contained in a grain that seems insignificant on the ground.

Now the poet has graduated from the world of the *bardd gwlad,* the *folk-poet,* to consider the composition of the microcosm and the macrocosm, drawing images to do so from his own environment. His vehicle, the Welsh language, accommodates this task with ease. To take one example of the vocabulary chosen by the bard, the word '*ddiddim*' 'insignificant' underlines the pedigree of formal Welsh. This word occurs in the Laws of Hywel Dda in the 10th century, and thereafter until the modern period in manuscripts and literary sources. It still occurs in the language today.

In these verses, the world presented is a world in which Man, God and Nature have not yet been rendered distinct or become dissociated, the one from the other. In the post-medieval world, reason assumes a role in promoting man as distinct from other elements in his immediate and wider environment. The premise 'cognito ergo sum', 'I think therefore I am', as postulated by Descartes (1596–1650), marks this juncture. Soon after, the idea in turn of Nature as something distinct is promoted in the thinking of the romantic period, and is well established in the poetry of Goethe (1749–1832). Isolated from Man and Nature in language and in philosophy as the modern period progresses, the notion of God soon begins to jar within the intellectual framework developed in post-medieval Europe, this leading ultimately to the growth of agnosticism and atheism. In *Bywyd a Byw* (*Life and Living*) as sung by B.T. Hopkins however, the notions of Man, Nature and God do not occur as such. The view of the cosmos expressed by B.T. Hopkins is an older, primary view that exists in parallel to the Cartesian world, a view that still enjoys vitality in the literary tradition of rural Wales in the 20th century.

When contemplating the world, B.T. Hopkins is bolstered by conviction, clear and confident. The point of departure for his description of the world is one of knowing and knowledge, his knowledge of the earth. This stands in contrast to early modern and modern European philosophy where the point of departure is typically one of incertitude, or presumed ignorance. Combining his knowledge of the earth with a literary tradition over a thousand years old, Hopkins, standing on Mynydd Bach mountain near Tregaron in West Wales, continues to sing in the tradition of Taliesin (6th century) who, when Christianity was still young, sang of the forces that animate the world.

This is not how B.T. Hopkins is remembered in local tradition in Ceredigion. Anecdotes surround his public appearances, and his wit was held in high regard. Hopkins was a lay preacher, and though he did not compete in the National *Eisteddfod,* he was invited to adjudicate at it. It is said that he wore two wigs, one during the week, and the other, noticeably redder, on Sundays.

In his poem *Bywyd* (*Life*) J.M. Edwards, a lifelong friend of B.T. Hopkins, also celebrates the forces that animate the world. However, these forces overwhelm him, and a struggle ensues between, as the poet perceives it, the civilised mind and the dark soul. He speaks of a wild beast driving its pagan impulses through his flesh, and drumming up the passions of a world of slime. These thoughts continue to play on J.M. Edwards' mind in the 1930s, when the poet was approaching his prime, before his repeated successes at the National *Eisteddfod* in the early 40s when he turned his attentions to the destruction wrought on civilisation by the machine. In the closing verses of *Bywyd* (*Life*), he resigns himself, briefly at least, to these forces that inhabit him. He speaks of excesses of passion and of rebellion that stirs the blood. These are things full of audacity, and nothing can withstand the galloping of their hooves.

There may be several reasons for the inner conflict to which J.M. Edwards was prey at one time in his career. We may ask however to what extent the puritanism prominent in certain circles in Wales during the poet's youth contributed to his unhappiness. As we have seen, this theme is dealt with in a little more detail in *Utopia and Dystopia*.

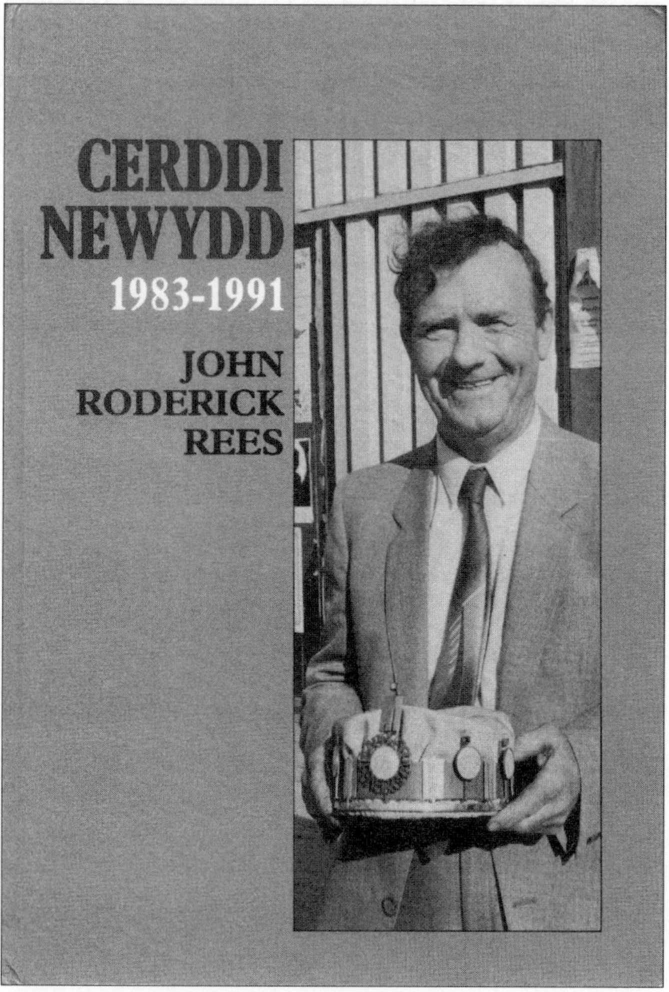
CERDDI
NEWYDD
1983-1991
JOHN
RODERICK
REES

John Roderick Rees – The Last of the Smallholders

From 2005 until 2007, short years before his death, I visited John Roderick Rees (1920–2009) several times at his home, a small-holding called Bear's Hill, in the parish of Bethania, near Tregaron, in central Ceredigion. In the early 1900s, the house had been a tavern called 'The Plough and Harrow', and now it stood on fifteen acres of land, that the poet and his father farmed for most of the 20th century.

The house was modestly furnished, largely unchanged over the decades, a tall grandfather clock solemnly measuring time in the kitchen, outhouses ringing the yard, a drawing room to the left, and a narrow staircase leading to the low rooms in the loft. The poet served tea in dainty china cups, and we conversed in our own tongue, heedless of the thickening night on the moor nearby. The kitchen wall was bedecked with ribbons, pictures of Welsh cobs, and prizes collected by the family for their involvement in the world of horse and plough in Ceredigion and beyond, over three generations. *Brenin Gwalia* was the most famous of the horses bred by the poet's father, a stallion born in 1934 that won major prizes in 1947 and 1948, and subject of one of the poet's better-known texts. During these visits, John Roderick Rees described himself as the last of the smallholders. The last time I saw him, we stood on a winter's night outside Bear's Hill, and briefly observed the stars. In this chapter, we delve into the terrestrial world he knew and wrote of.

John Roderick Rees began writing poetry at an early age, composing his first sonnets at the age of seventeen. After leaving school in the late thirties, he remained at home in Bear's Hill to farm the land. He was an only son, and chose not to join the army during the second world war. His stance as a conscientious objector caused him no little social discomfort. When the war had ended, John Roderick Rees made another decision that illustrates the independence of mind that characterises the man. Aged twenty-seven, he enrolled in the University of Wales, Aberystwyth, and read for a degree in Welsh and English. Some years later, he was appointed head of the department of Welsh at Tregaron Grammar School, a few miles from his home in Bethania, a post he held for much of the rest of his working life.

John Roderick Rees published three volumes of poetry, *Cerddi'r Ymylon* (*Poems from the Margins*) (1959), *Cerddi* (*Poems*) (1984), a *Cherddi Newydd* (*New Poems*) (1992). He won the crown at the national *Eisteddfod* two years running, in Llanbedr-Pont-Steffan in 1984, and in Rhyl in 1985. From the mid-seventies until 1981, he took time off from work to nurse his foster mother Jane Mary Walters who was suffering from dementia. After his retirement, he remained in Bear's Hill until his death in 2009. John Roderick Rees lost both his parents prematurely. His mother was thirty when she passed away, leaving her two-and-a-half-year-old son, and her husband. His father died soon after his fiftieth birthday.

The work of John Roderick Rees is informed by a strong sense of aesthetic and literary values. The subject of aesthetics *per se* is not visited in the work, nor in the work of his fellows, and there is here no extended discussion or questioning of poetics in general, no striving to compose a definitive *ars poetica,* no creative agenda that seeks to promote a given way of thinking, perhaps to the detriment of another. As a result, and no doubt in ways subconscious, there is an acceptance of inherited literary and aesthetic values regarding verse and poetry, values according to which the writing of verse and poetry is an earnest and elevated pursuit.

This unspoken premise leads in turn to preferences for a particular style of writing. Poetry here is synonymous with structure and discipline. An extensive literary vocabulary will characterise a good poet. A poem should enrich the reader's understanding of the world, and as such the reader is, arguably, indebted to the poet in some way. Furthermore, the art of poetry is an old and venerable one, and writing within this tradition, the poet is aware of a tradition he is required, if only by his own modesty, to respect.

John Roderick Rees, as with others of the Ceredigion poets, writes poetry that is in no way surreal, iconoclastic or avant-garde, pious or metaphysical, nostalgic or romantic, virtuoso or extrovert, infatuated or passionate. All these things excluded, we find space to consider the realism of his writing, its humaneness, and its modernity. For example, in *Calan Gaeaf* (*Winter's Eve*), we are introduced to Siâms yr Hafod, a small-holder who farms forty acres of clay, a heavy burden for two pairs of hands. The sheaves he harvests are coarse and brittle, reflecting the nature of the soil, but the poet asks us to show Siâms some compassion, and to respect his resilience on the mountain.

Official art is part of the apparel of a nation. Work cut from the cloth of this apparel receives recognition and is commended. The artists and writers whose work offers the nation images and symbols in which to recognise itself are given status within the establishment, and become heralds of the national discourse. The work of John Roderick Rees is not representative of the official art or discourse of the time in Wales that had begun to develop by 1960. This discourse is better enshrined in *Gwreiddiau* (*Roots*), for example, a volume of verse by a man called Gwenallt whose name is firmly established in the canon and nomenclature of Welsh literature in the third quarter of the 20th century.

In *Gwreiddiau* we discover a political discourse built on the pillars of language, nation and Christianity as an expression of civilisation. These three things are perceived as being under threat, and steps to ensure their survival become a matter of urgency. *Gwreiddiau* (*Roots*) was published in 1959, the same year as *Cerddi'r Ymylon* (*Poems from the Periphery*) by John Roderick Rees. The volume is aptly named, but, owing partly to the fact that it does not contain an overt and direct politico-cultural message, the book remained on the margins.

John Roderick Rees writes in praise of Gwenallt and his vision (*Cerddi,* pp 108-9), referring appropriately to his work as a 'nationalist Christian crusade'. The last of the smallholders, a bard from Bethania, John Roderick Rees embarks himself on no such idealistic crusade. In his work he pays homage to the farm-hand, the maid, the elderly widow, the nameless old, and to the common people. Whereas Gwenallt beats the drum of Owain Glyndŵr whose revolution in the early 1400s challenged the crown, and of Bishop William Morgan whose seminal translation of the Welsh Bible was published in 1588, John Roderick Rees in *Cerddi'r Ymylon* (*Poems from the Periphery*) writes, often austerely, of poor men such as Siams yr Hafod and Dai Penbanc. Without the angry rhetoric of Gwenallt's *Gwreiddiau,* who writes of abstracts and principles, John Roderick Rees seems close in his humility to the basic tenents of Christianity.

Published in 1959, *Cerddi'r Ymylon* (*Poems from the Periphery*) marks the beginning of John Roderick Rees' publishing career, but it is a career that falters and seems to grind to a halt. In 1960, the poet wrote *Unigedd* (*Solitude*) and submitted it to the National *Eisteddfod.* Of twenty-nine entries received in its category that year, a long poem in any metre, known as *pryddest* in Welsh, *Unigedd* was deemed one of three worthy of the crown. The prize however was awarded to W.J. Gruffydd of Ffair Rhos. In the 1964 *Eisteddfod* in Swansea, according to one of the adjudicators, Sir T.H. Parry Williams, Rees' *Ffynhonnau* (*Sources*) was the best entry in the *pryddest* category. Others of the jury disagreed, and again favour failed to shine on the last of the smallholders from Bethania.

After 1964, John Roderick Rees ceased to enter for the *Eisteddfod.* A note in *Cerddi,* in the biographical paragraph, overtly states his disillusionment. His second collection *Cerddi John Roderick Rees* (*The Poems of John Roderick Rees*) did not appear until 1984, and this is where the two long poems *Unigedd* (1960) and *Ffynhonnau* (1964) are to be found. Alongside these two texts, and occasional verse written between 1965 and 1984, the contents of *Cerddi'r Ymylon* are reprinted in full. The poet intended this collection to be his epitaph, but more was to come. In 1984, John Roderick Rees won the crown in the National *Eisteddfod* with the poem *Llygaid* (*Eyes*), and the following year with *Glannau* (*Banks*), a poem inspired by the time he spent nursing his foster-mother.

This double success at national level meant several things. The contents of *Cerddi* (*Poems*) (1984) was now much less than fully representative of the poet's work than had been intended. Also, thanks to the author's two *Eisteddfod* crowns, all his work now became the object of some interest. This led to a third volume, *Cerddi Newydd,* published in 1992, a book that contains *Llygaid* (*Eyes*) (1984) and *Glannau* (*Banks*) 1985, as well as some new material, three of the most significant poems being *Yn Nyddiau'r Pasg* (*Easter Week*), *Gwaedd y Bechgyn* (*The Young Men's Shout*), and *Sul o Ragfyr, Bethania 1987* (*Sunday in December*).

However, in this third volume, as in the second, together

with the best of the poet's writing, there are a number of less memorable poems, some little more than notes and jottings. Furthermore, the poet received no editorial advice regarding the inclusion or exclusion of controversial political pieces such as *Moliant i Ronald Reagan* (*In Praise of Ronald Reagan*), or *Margaret Thatcher* in which he praises the political leader's 'Oxfordian intellect'. Approaching the work of John Roderick Rees therefore, we find a mixed corpus in need of some editing. A selection of the poems from the three extant volumes would facilitate a reading of the work.

If issues surrounding editorial practice contribute to the clouding of the message in the work of John Roderick Rees, this message is also compromised at times by poetic form and structure. In 1855, the American Walt Whitman published *Leaves of Grass,* a revolutionary work that ushers in the epoch of free verse. Rhyming couplets, and other forms of rhyme, continued to be practiced for another century in English and other European languages. After 1900 however, rhyme begins to fall from favour. During the years between the two World Wars, rhyming verse survives in tandem with free verse. After the second World War, it becomes archaic and banal. In Welsh, however, and in the work of John Roderick Rees, the practice of rhyming verse continues beyond the 1960s. Indeed, as much as two thirds of the work in the 1992 volume *Cerddi Newydd* (*New Poems*) makes use of rhyme in one way or another.

John Roderick Rees, it should be noted, did not compose verse in *cynghanedd,* strict metre poetry, as did the bards of southern Ceredigion, amongst them the Cilie brothers and Dic Jones, for example. In general, however, *cynghanedd* in our period finds fewer practitioners in the harsher Tregaron uplands in mid-Ceredigion than in the lusher south near the Teifi estuary. *Cynghanedd,* very much in vogue in Wales for much of the 20th century, is sonorous and full-sounding, working best when recited. To say that in *cynghanedd*, Welsh poets find uplifting and ingenious ways to express commonplace things is not untrue. In translation however, the music of the original lost, the tension of the lines undone, and Welsh poems written in *cynghanedd* remind one of *The Albatross* by Charles Baudelaire whose 'giant wings prevent him from walking'. Translating the poetry of John Roderick Rees tends to produce the opposite effect. In translation, the banal rhymes that detract from the modernist spirit of the original texts are discarded, and the spirit of the poetry shines through. Ironically perhaps, a poet who inhabited the margins for most of his lifetime can hope to emerge in translation to cast a shadow over those who enjoyed acclaim in their own time.

In *Y Llwybrau Gynt* (*The Paths of Old*), he recalls how the pioneers of the upland crofts cut hay on the hilly meadow, stacked it then by the tidy cow-house, and breathed its sweet nectar in the manger, hay that helped see them through the hungry winter under a shroud of drift-snow. In *Y Winllan* (*Vineyard*), we read in verse a history in several parts of lord, land and tenant. The series begins in the nineteenth century, when the steward comes to survey the land, waving his blank page over the commonage like the shadow of kestrel's wings, and chains the mountain to the new laws of enclosure. Once the purchase of commonage has been set in ink, the manor becomes a lair for the feasting of the idle, while the river bank, where an unhurried countryman saves his hay, falls into oblivion on an attorney's desk. Now the mountain belongs to the mansion, and a trench is dug on the parish boundaries to keep the common people out. Despite the claws of fate however, the poor man is given consent to construct his *tŷ unnos*, his one-night house, somewhere in the virgin acres high on the mountain. And so it comes to pass that the inhospitable uplands become home to a new community of hill-farmers.

As I left Bear's Hill on a November evening in 2006, John Roderick Rees, the last of the native Welsh smallholders to ply both pen and plough, stood in a long trench-coat observing the stars. His hair seemed black despite his advanced years, and he used no stick to walk. '*Mae honna yn un danbaid,*' he said, pointing to an un-named celestial body – 'that's a bright one there'. And before I drove away into the new century, I heard him add, ever true to the bonds of kith and kin; '*cofiwch fi at eich mam*', 'remember me to your mother'. This book began during my visits to John Roderick Rees in the years before his death, and so it ends now, almost ten years later.

Bibliography

I

Books of Poetry by Ceredigion Bards

- *Y Tir Pell a Cherddi Eraill*, J.M. Edwards, Lloyd ap Hefin Aberdar 1933
- *Cerddi Pum Mlynedd*, J.M. Edwards, Gomer 1938
- *Cerddi'r Bwthyn*, Dewi Emrys, Gwasg Aberystwyth Press 1948
- *Caniadau Isgarn*, Richard Davies (Isgarn), National Library of Wales Press 1949
- *Cerddi Isfoel*, Dafydd Jones (Isfoel), Gwasg Aberystwyth Press 1958
- *Cerddi'r Ymylon*, John Roderick Rees, Cymdeithas Llyfrau Aberystwyth 1959
- *Cerddi Ffair Rhos*, Evan Jenkins, Gwasg Aberystwyth Press 1959
- *Agor Grwn*, Dic Jones, Gwasg John Penry Press 1960
- *Ffenestri a Cherddi Eraill*, W.J. Gruffydd, Gwasg Aberystwyth 1961
- *Cerddi Hamdden*, J.M. Edwards, Llyfrau'r Dryw 1962
- *Rhwng Cyrn yr Aradr*, J.R. Jones, Llyfrau'r Dryw 1964
- *Cerddi Alun Cilie*, Alun Jones (Alun Cilie), Gwasg John Penry Press 1964
- *Ail Gerddi Isfoel*, Dafydd Jones (Isfoel), Gomer 1965
- *Wedi'r Storom*, Dewi Emrys, Gomer 1965
- *Yr Arloeswr a Cherddi Eraill*, Dafydd Jones (Ffair Rhos), Gwasg John Penry Press 1965
- *Cerddi ac Ysgrifau* S.B. Jones, Gomer 1966
- *Sŵn y Malu*, T. Llew Jones, Gomer 1967
- *Cerddi y Pren Gwyn*, Ifan Jones, Cymdeithas Llyfrau Ceredigion 1968
- *Caneuon Cynhaeaf*, Dic Jones, Gwasg John Penry Press 1969
- *Cerddi J.R. Talybont*, J.R. Jones, Gomer 1970
- *Cerddi Ddoe a Heddiw*, J.M. Edwards, Gwasg Gee Press 1975
- *Awen Ysgafn Y Cilie* ed. Gerallt Jones, Gomer 1976
- *Cerddi Pentalar*, Alun Cilie, Gomer 1976
- *Rhos Helyg a Cherddi Eraill*, Ben T. Hopkins, Cyhoeddiadau Modern Cymreig 1976
- *Storom Awst*, Dic Jones, Gomer 1978

- *Cerddi Cwm Eleri,* J.R. Jones, Gomer 1980
- *Cerddi John Roderick Rees,* Cymdeithas Lyfrau Aberystwyth 1984
- *Sgubo'r Storws,* Dic Jones, Gomer 1986
- *Canu yn Iach,* T. Llew Jones, Gomer 1987
- *Cerddi Newydd* 1983–1991, John Roderick Rees, Barddas 1992
- *Crafion Medi,* J.R. Jones, Gomer 1992
- *Cadw Golwg,* Dic Jones, Gwasg Gwynedd Press 2005
- *Golwg Arall,* Dic Jones, Gomer 2009
- *Yr Un Hwyl a'r Un Wylo – Cerddi Gwlad Dic Jones,* Dic Jones, Gomer 2011

II

Selected Secondary and Related Literature

- *Ar Gefn ei Geffyl,* Richard Phillips, Cymdeithas Lyfrau Ceredigion 1969
- *Ar Lethrau Ffair Rhos,* W. Jones-Edwards, Cymdeithas Lyfrau Ceredigion 1963
- *Atgofion Cardi,* Thomas Richards, Cymdeithas Lyfrau Ceredigion 1960
- *Atgofion Dau Grefftwr,* Dan Davies and William J. Hughes, Cymdeithas Lyfrau Ceredigion 1963
- *Ar Ymylon Cors Caron,* Evan Jones, Cymdeithas Lyfrau Ceredigion 1967
- *Bro a Bywyd – Beirdd y Mynydd Bach,* ed. Emyr Edwards, Barddas 1999
- *Bro a Bywyd – T. Llew Jones,* ed. John Meirion Jones, Barddas 2010
- *Bugail y Bryn,* Maelona, Y Cymro 1917
- *Cau'r Tiroedd Comin,* David Thomas, Gwasg y Brython 1952
- *Coelion Cymru,* Evan Isaac, Y Clwb Llyfrau Cymraeg 1938
- *Dewi Emrys,* Eluned Phillips, Gomer 1971
- *Fy Mhobol i,* T. Llew Jones, Gomer 2002
- *Ffynnonloyw,* Maelona, Gomer 1939
- *Hen Ŷd y Wlad,* Dafydd Jones (Isfoel), Gomer 1966
- *Le Quêteur de Mémoire,* Pierre Jakez Hélias, France Loisirs 1990
- *La Fin des Paysans,* Henri Mendras, Actes Sud 1984 (1967)
- *Lewis Morris and the Cardiganshire Mines,* David Bick and Philip Wyn Davies, The National Library of Wales 1994

- *Morwyr y Cilie,* Jon Meirion Jones, Barddas 2002
- *My People,* Caradog Evans, Seren 2003 (1915)
- *O Ffair Rhos i'r Maen Llog,* W.J. Gruffydd, Gomer 2003
- *O Gwmpas Pumlumon,* J.M. Davies, Cymdeithas Lyfrau Ceredigion 1966
- *Os Hoffech Wybod,* Dic Jones, Gwasg Gwynedd 2010
- *Rhagor o Atgofion Cardi,* Thomas Richards, Cymdeithas Lyfrau Ceredigion 1963
- *Teulu'r Cilie,* Jon Meirion Jones, Barddas 1999
- *The Agricultural Community in South-West Wales at the turn of the 20th Century,* David Jenkins, University of Wales Press, 1971
- *Y Gwron o Dalgarreg,* ed. T. Llew Jones, Cymdeithas Llyfrau Ceredigion 1967
- *Yr Aradr Gymreig,* Ffransis Payne, University of Wales Press 1954

